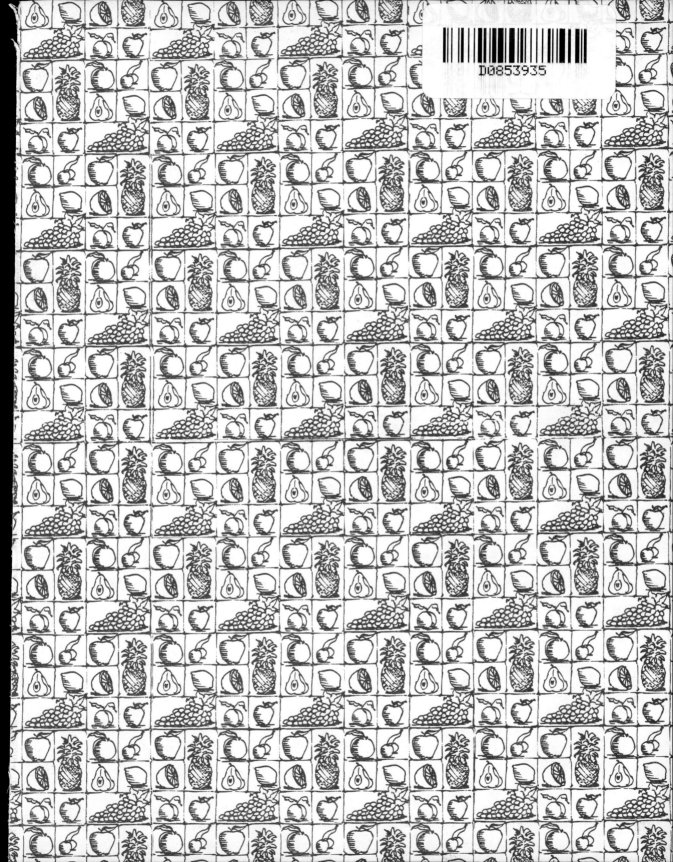

These recipes are from professional chefs. Our editors have tediously checked each ingredient and each instruction in every recipe to make certain ingredients specified are generally available and instructions understandable. We hope we have achieved this goal for you. The Culinary Complements section at the back of this cookbook is a special section on wine selections and cooking hints.

Here's to enjoying good food and wine, eating, drinking, and talking about it!

The Publisher

Chefs' Secrets
from
Great Restaurants
in
Georgia

Marmac Publishing Company, Inc.
Atlanta, Georgia

Copyright© 1983 Marmac Publishing Company, Inc.
6303 Barfield Road, Suite 208, Atlanta, GA 30328

ISBN: 0-939944-06-5
Library of Congress Number: 82-062613

Recipe Editor, Jean Thwaite
Editors, Diana Nicholson and Susan Smith
Book design by Pezzutti's Studio, Atlanta, Georgia
Illustrations by Jan Chaput, Atlanta, Georgia
Cover photography by Conway-Carter Photography, Atlanta, Georgia

Cover photograph props: wineglass and casserole dish courtesy of Tiffany & Co.;
stainless-steel pot courtesy of Someone's in the Kitchen, Atlanta, Georgia;
pilaster courtesy of The Wrecking Bar, Atlanta, Georgia.

Manufactured in the United States of America

Restaurants featured are members of the Georgia Hospitality and Travel Association

TABLE OF CONTENTS

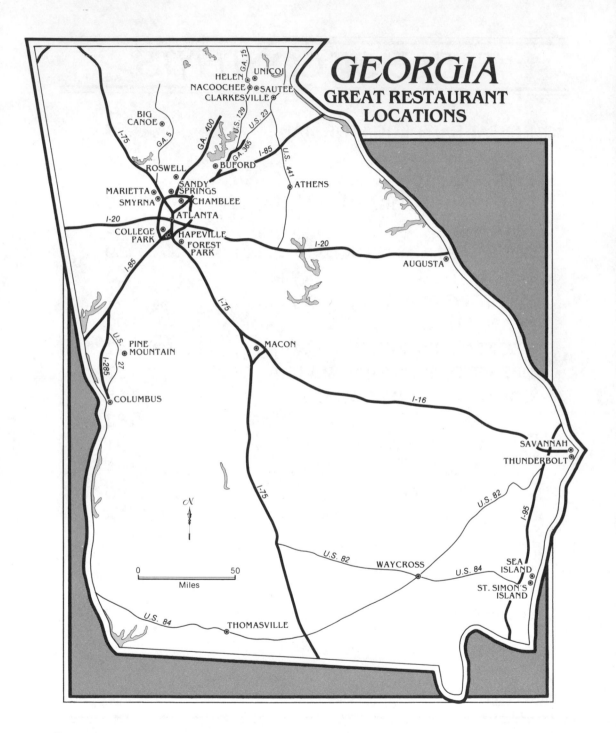

GEORGIA
GREAT RESTAURANT
LOCATIONS

HELEN · UNICOI
NACOOCHEE · · SAUTEE
CLARKESVILLE

BIG
CANOE

ROSWELL
BUFORD

SANDY
SPRINGS
MARIETTA · · CHAMBLEE
SMYRNA

ATHENS

ATLANTA
COLLEGE · HAPEVILLE
PARK FOREST
PARK

AUGUSTA

PINE
MOUNTAIN

MACON

COLUMBUS

SAVANNAH
THUNDERBOLT

WAYCROSS

SEA
ISLAND

ST. SIMON'S
ISLAND

0   50
Miles

THOMASVILLE

FOREWORD

In commemoration of Georgia's semiquincentennial birthday, (250th), **The Georgia Hospitality and Travel Association** (Georgia's Hotel/Motel, Restaurant, and Travel Industry Association) is proud to present this cookbook as a celebration of Georgia's fine dining. In order to do this we realize we must share some of our most valued secrets, and Georgia chefs from the mountains to the seacoast, through the piedmont and the plains have answered in this book the questions they so frequently received from visitors about their special dishes.

Dining in Georgia is a culinary adventure — offering everything from fresh seacoast delicacies, to family-style mountain barbecue, to cosmopolitan Atlanta elegance and international cuisine.

The quality and rich diversity are reflected in the recipes submitted by selected chefs from some of Georgia's best restaurants.

William Schemmel's introduction gives a unique history to dining and foods in the many regions of the state, from colonial days in Savannah to contemporary times.

The recipes are arranged in categories of Appetizers, Soups, Salads, and Sauces; Meats; Poultry; Seafood; Vegetables and Breads; Desserts, Pastries, and Beverages; and indexed by category, recipe, and restaurant. The Georgia map shows all the towns where restaurants are participating. The final section entitled Culinary Complements provides advice on wines and entertaining, recipes for sauces and stocks, and a glossary defining common terms used in this book.

Join with Georgia in her 250th year and sample some of her great dining treasures presented for you here.

Bon Appétit!

Robert R. King
President
Georgia Hospitality and
Travel Association

"He may live without books,—what is knowledge but grieving?
He may live without hope,—what is hope but deceiving?
He may live without love,—what is passion but pining?
But where is the man that can live without dining?"

OWEN MEREDITH

INTRODUCTION

Dining out has been a cherished Georgia custom since the founding days of King George III's 13th American colony. No sooner had General James Edward Oglethorpe and his sea-weary colonists come ashore at Savannah on 12 February 1733, than Chief Tomo-Chi-Chi of the Yamacraws bade his subjects prepare an extravagant feast of welcome.

Deer and wild boar succulently barbecued over huge open pits were served the awestruck guests, along with bountiful platters of oysters, clams, shrimp, turkey, roasted corn, wild berries, honey, nuts, and seeds. When the feasting was done, the Yamacraws performed festive tribal dances and were treated, in turn, to English country dances accompanied by instruments strange to the Indians' ears.

Given leave by the hospitable Tomo-Chi-Chi, the English laid out Savannah on a grid, modeled after Peking, which miraculously survives today. In their gardens, the colonists planted figs, grape vines, plums, indigo, spices, beans, and other fruits from Europe. From across the Atlantic they brought their taste for English roasted beef, puddings, trifles, and fruit cakes.

Over the past 250 years, these culinary roots have intertwined with the tastes of the Greek, Italian, Jewish, Chinese, German, French, black, and American Indian peoples and more than a score of others who have lent their own spice to Georgia's cosmopolitan cookpot.

EARLY DAYS IN SAVANNAH

During the first half of the 19th century, Savannah bloomed as the port through which Georgia cotton flowed to the mills of Liverpool and Boston. Wealthy planters, merchants, and shippers set a pattern of gracious dining that remains a Savannah hallmark today. Dinner parties in the lovely English regency and federal period homes always included an array of richly sauced meats and fish, soups and rare delicacies, sweets and imported wines.

While fine dining was conducted in the great homes, Savannah's early taverns were the haunts of seamen. The city's famous Pirates' House is believed to be Georgia's oldest restaurant and tavern. Built in 1754, alongside Trustees' Garden near the waterfront, the establishment was a popular venue for sailors and pirates. Captain Flint, the villainous cutthroat of Robert Louis Stevenson's *Treasure Island* is said to still haunt an upstairs room where he died. These days, the Pirates' House, a fascinating maze of more than 20 nautically decorated dining rooms, is one of Georgia's best known and busiest restaurants.

LOCAL FAVORITES

Rice, brought to Georgia on merchant ships from the Orient, flourished in the marshy tidal waters of the Altamaha River. Although rice cultivation perished with the Civil War, the fluffy grain retains a place of honor on our plates. Diners at Savannah's best restaurants frequently find a mound of the Mother City's famous red rice, piquantly married with green peppers, onions, diced ham, tomato sauce, and spices beside their shrimp, oysters, and flounder.

Seafoods are the crown jewels of Georgia's coast. Crabmeat and shrimp are the heart of savory gumbos, bisques, and she-crab soup. They are draped in cheese sauce au gratin, deviled, Newburged, and simply and tastily boiled and steamed. Oysters, likewise, come in a variety of dress, but the oyster roast is ritual. Bushels of fresh mollusks are spread on iron racks, covered with dampened seaweed or burlap and coaxed gently open by the glowing coals of a barbecue pit.

THE GOLDEN ISLES

Georgia wears her Golden Isles like a grand duchess does her diamonds, some like Cumberland and Little St. Simons remaining cloaked in primeval mystery, and others such as Sea Island, Jekyll, and St. Simons becoming popular vacation destinations.

General Oglethorpe and the English came to St. Simons shortly after founding Savannah, but vacationers didn't discover the healing qualities of its ocean breezes until late in the last century. Before 1924, when the first wooden causeway connected the island with Brunswick, visitors came to St. Simons on the ferry boats *Emmeline* and *Hessie*. They stayed in beachside boardinghouses and savored the glories of freshly netted seafoods just as we do today.

Separated from St. Simons by a narrow estuary is Sea Island, a resort haven since 1928. Guests still count dining among the biggest blessings of a vacation here.

In the late 1880s, Jekyll Island caught the eye of a group of wealthy Eastern families. Those who were invited to this plush cocoon were privy to a lifestyle that has now largely vanished. Chefs from New York and France prepared extravagant dinner parties in the island's opulent "cottages." French champagne, caviar, pâté de foie gras, barons of beef, oysters, and all manner of rare delicacies highlighted these affairs.

Brunswick, the gateway to these islands, was also known for its superb kitchen and beautifully appointed dining rooms in the old rambling wooden Oglethorpe hotel with its turrets and wide verandahs, since razed for a department store.

THE HEARTLAND

Savannah had scarcely begun to rise above Yamacraw Bluff when restless Georgians started moving away from the coast into the forested upper reaches of the Savannah River and further west into the wild unknown of the state's heartland. New towns were graced with classical and patriotic names: Athens, Augusta, Madison, Washington, Jefferson, Monroe, Monticello, and Lincolnton (honoring an English town, not our sixteenth president). Milledgeville was the only town ever specifically planned as a state capital, and nobly served that role from 1806 to 1868, when Atlanta was given the honor.

On their dining tables, the up-country Georgians blended their coastal rice, English beef and puddings, and Indian corn, fruit, and berries with fish they found in rivers and streams, and venison, boar, and other wild game from the forests. Until the end of the 18th century, buffalo roamed this region. Virginians who came south during the Revolution introduced buckwheat cakes, wheaten flour, loaf sugar, and a variety of pastries, cakes, and sweets made from molasses.

Peaches, with which Georgia has become synonymous, immigrated to our shores from China, and grew to perfection in the warm climate and rich earth of Georgia's midlands. In all their wisdom, the ancient Chinese never dreamt that anything could be as delicious as a peach cobbler baked to bubbling brown excellence by a Georgia farm wife. Fort Valley in Peach County is the epicenter of Georgia's peach industry, but come midsummer this luscious fruit is enjoyed in pies, cakes, preserves, glazes, even cold soup, all over our state.

BARBECUE, BRUNSWICK STEW, AND OTHER SOUTHERN TREATS

Early travelers could always be certain of warm hospitality from plantation families eager for a bit of news and gossip from the outside world. How fortunate were those weary wanderers who arrived in time for a barbecue. Among the most important social events of ante-bellum Georgia life and a festive occasion for families to gather for many miles around, a barbecue centered around whole pigs slowly roasting on spits over huge piles of glowing coals. Guests could also look forward to thick gumbos and Brunswick stew, smoked hams, quail, pheasant, fried chicken, beaten biscuits, cornbread, Sally Lunn bread, pies, cakes, and sweets.

Georgia barbecue nearly always means pork rather than beef. The succulent meat is draped in a thick, red, sweet-piquant sauce made with ketchup, vinegar, Worcestershire sauce, dry mustard, garlic, lemon juice, and butter. Every Georgia barbecue chef has his or her own special touches. Consequently no two sauces are ever exactly alike, and the joy of sampling barbecue in dozens of locale is all the more exciting.

Georgians would no more omit Brunswick stew from their plate of barbecue than they would go about during the day wearing only one shoe. Whether it originated in Brunswick in Georgia, Brunswick County in Virginia, or someplace else, this thick, savory stew, usually prepared in big iron pots, is a satisfying blend of chopped chicken and pork, onions, potatoes, tomatoes, corn, butterbeans, celery, and spices. A well-rounded barbecue plate will also include slices of white bread, pickles, cole slaw, baked beans, and french fries.

Country hams, smoke-cured and rubbed with just the right combination of salt, spices, and sugar, are another Georgia treasure. And along with these specialties, Georgia and the South have made their mark on the culinary world with chicken, fried a crisp golden brown.

Ask any true southern cook how to cook "Southern Fried Chicken," and you'll be told straight off that all that is required is a plump chicken fryer — two to two-and-a-half pounds, properly cut up, washed, and dried, rolled in peppered and salted flour, and fried for about twenty minutes (ten minutes on each side) in cooking oil just deep enough to barely cover the pieces.

TAVERNS AND TOWNS IN THE CLASSIC SOUTH

Travelers who failed to find sanctuary at a private home could take respite from the rigors of the road at inns and taverns that sprang up on stagecoach routes connecting the coast with the new towns of the interior. Some were luxurious, with delicious foods prepared over an open hearth, feather beds, and even entertainment by traveling musicians and players.

The Eagle Tavern at Watkinsville in northeast Georgia was one of the most famous lodgings of its day. Opened at the beginning of the nineteenth century, the handsome two-story frame building was furnished with pewter and china imported from England, and furniture made by local craftspeople. Guests could always be certain of roasted meats, fresh breads, and stews bubbling in iron pots over the hearth.

Further north, near Toccoa, Travelers Rest began receiving guests around the 1830s, and served typical southern foods such as baked hams and poultry, fried pies, and hot spiced apple cider. Like many early inns, the two-story clapboard structure, with its brick and stone chimneys, was also a plantation home, as well as a post office and store. It has now been restored and opened to the public as a museum.

Another ante-bellum town, Madison, east of Atlanta, is one of Georgia's most beautiful, graced with many white-columned mansions that even General Sherman found too lovely to burn.

Like Savannah, Augusta was planned in 1735 by General Oglethorpe and the original Georgia colonists. During the late eighteenth century, it served briefly as our state capital, and still preserves many lovely souvenirs of its long and colorful history. However, the city is now best known around the world as the home of the annual Masters Golf Tournament, which was first played on the Augusta National Golf Course in 1934. Visitors continue to enjoy the excellent southern cuisine and deluxe accommodations in the multitude of fine resorts, hotels, inns, and restaurants.

Macon, middle Georgia's metropolis, can trace its roots back to the War of 1812, when it was a mustering point for patriots bound to vanquish the British one more time. Laid out as a town in 1823, the city developed as a shipping port on the Ocmulgee River, a railroad hub and distribution point for middle Georgia cotton. Sidney Lanier, Georgia's best known poet, lived here and his cottage is open to the public. The city's tree-shaded streets are graced with many fine ante-bellum and Victorian mansions, and its restaurants are noted for the quality of their southern cooking. Fried chicken, southern vegetables, and fried catfish with hushpuppies are nowhere finer than at Macon's renowned restaurants. Hushpuppies, the story goes, got their name from early hunters, who threw bits of fried cornmeal to quiet restless dogs.

ATLANTA, THE CAPITAL

Dining in Atlanta mirrors the diversity of this booming, internationally minded metropolis. The capital city's southern cooks zealously preserve the handed-down traditions of chicken fried to a golden turn, biscuits light as nimbus clouds, greens simmered with hambone, and juicy cobblers created from Georgia's famous peaches.

Name your culinary preference, and Atlanta's fine restaurants are certain to have a pleasing answer. Such has not always been the case.

The city was settled in the north Georgia wilderness by Scottish, Irish, and English railroad laborers, who felt most comfortable amid the simple pleasures of taverns and saloons. One such tavern willed its name to what is now our most affluent and fashionable neighborhood.

In the 1830s, Henry Irby, an enterprising South Carolinian, built a tavern and grocery store at what is now the busy intersection of West Paces Ferry and Roswell Roads. When out in the nearby woods one day, Irby felled an impressive deer, and he then nailed the deer's head to a post in front of his establishment. It became known as the Buck's Head Tavern, and the area for several miles around has been called Buckhead ever since.

As the city rebuilt and flourished after the Civil War, taverns assumed a polished new elegance. Two in-places of the period were Muhlenbrink's and P. J. Kenney's, which were reborn in Underground Atlanta in the 1970s.

The first hotel boom followed the flow of northern entrepreneurs into the city. In 1870 the Kimball House boasted a frescoed and mirrored dining room, offering oysters from the coast and violinists from New York.

When the Piedmont Hotel opened in 1903 at Forsyth, Peachtree, and Luckie Streets, proud Atlantans conferred their ultimate accolade — it was our "New York Hotel," with an uptown menu to match: blue point oysters, Little Neck clams, braised sweetbreads, roast quail, turkey with oyster dressing, prime roast beef, and Detroit River white fish.

In 1924, the Atlanta Biltmore, fashionably away from the noisy downtown business district, wooed guests to marble terraces, landscaped gardens, and smart dinners of fillet of kingfish fin de siecle, medallion of sweetbread Monaco, tomatoes madrilene, potatoes persilees, mousseline of fresh mushrooms, and a dessert called "Fantasy Atlanta."

On the site of the original governor's mansion, the Henry Grady Hotel opened that same year and was quickly adopted by members of the Georgia General Assembly. Wild pig suppers were held in the Grady's upper reaches the night before the Assembly opened and remained a firmly entrenched tradition until the wrecking ball tolled the hotel's demise in the 1970s.

During the Grady's prime, Atlanta couples came down to the Dogwood Room to enjoy steaks and shrimp cocktails, and dance to the big-band orchestra. The Rainbow Roof of the Ansley (later Dinkler-Plaza) Hotel on Forsyth Street was another popular venue for dining and dancing.

Some of Atlanta's most legendary restaurants were born during the Thirties. Created by Frances Virginia Wikle Whitaker, the Frances Virginia Tea Room on Peachtree Street across from Davison's Department Store was the landmark for white-gloved downtown shoppers until the early 1960s. The cuisine was southern gourmet. Shrimp salad, hot turkey on egg bread with giblet gravy, and squash souffle were among the many elegant dishes. But the Frances Virginia was most widely acclaimed for the glory of its fried chicken, which was given an even golden-brown crust by a secret ingredient — potato flour — in the breading.

Several other fine restaurants who also opened their doors at this time still remain today as landmarks in the city's dining. The middle sixties saw the advent of cabarets and supper clubs, and a decade later came the stylish bistros and sophisticated continental menus and casual ambiance.

Now Metro Atlanta's 2-million residents, and visitors from all parts of the world, may savor cuisines from France and Italy; Greece and Spain; China, Korea, Japan, and Thailand; from Mexico and Latin America; California and Texas; New England, New York, and Louisiana's Cajun country while still maintaining its heritage of southern cooking and soul food.

Curiously enough, "southern cooking" and "soul cooking" are virtually identical. Questioned about this phenomenon, one restaurateur smiled mischievously and said: "Ain't a bit of difference. If white hands make it, it's southern homecooking, and if black hands make it, it's soul." Many cooks delineate the difference between southern and soul as a matter of refinement. They point to complex vegetable casseroles, souffles, and quail and pheasant with cream and wine sauces, as true "southern cuisine," while such simple favorites as turnip greens, fried chicken, baked sweet potatoes, and cornbread are "country southern" or "soul."

Atlanta's new-found appreciation of diverse ethnic cuisines and American regional cooking styles has spread across the state. Larger cities like Savannah, Macon, Columbus, Augusta, and Albany offer a wide variety of dining experiences. Even smaller cities and towns enjoy Mexican, Chinese, Italian, and other international dishes.

Not that we love southern cooking any less. It is simply that a flood of fellow Americans, Europeans, Canadians, Latin Americans, Asians, and Orientals has shown us that there is, after all, life beyond fried chicken and beaten biscuits.

UP TO THE NORTHERN MOUNTAINS

The earth reaches up to brush against the skies in the serene and timeless mountain lands of northern Georgia. Waterfalls plunge out of the forested high country to join forces with rivers dashing relentlessly toward the sea.

The city-weary in search of renewal come to these mountains to fish, swim, paddle a canoe, backpack the Appalachian Trail, drink in the scenery, and enjoy some of Georgia's most wonderful homecooking.

Whetted by highland air as crisp and fresh as new white wine, appetites here often seem as limitless as the landscape. To assuage such bountiful needs, family-style dining takes on prodigious new dimensions, where tables are laden with bottomless platters of country ham, fried chicken, chicken and dumplings, mustard greens, collard greens, turnip greens, squash casseroles, stewed corn, corn bread, slaws, homemade pickles, cobblers, and cakes.

Hospitality is an old and venerable tradition in the mountains. For more than fifty years, Tallulah Gorge was a summer vacation and honeymoon retreat whose fame rivaled Niagara Falls for southern visitors. Guests arrived by special train and stayed in big rambling hotels. Adventurous types could hike down into the gorge and stand spellbound by a half-dozen waterfalls along the racing Tallulah River. Mealtimes were always special occasions, time to discuss the day's discoveries over broiled mountain trout, bass and bream, and pies and cakes created from apples picked that same day.

Habersham County is the heart of Georgia's apple country, and motorists entering the town of Cornelia are greeted by an apple-shaped monument and a sign that proclaims: "Habersham County: Home of the Big Red Apple."

First-time visitors are always startled when they come over a rise and see the red roofs and flower boxes, the glockenspiel and Alpine architecture of the White County village of Helen. The once quiet town went European about a decade ago. Today travelers may experience Old Country sauerbraten, schnitzels, wursts, apple strudels, tortes, and marzipan at charming Bavarian-style restaurants.

America's first gold rush took place near Dahlonega in 1828, more than twenty years before the more famous California strikes. After seeing the Gold Museum in the old Lumpkin County Courthouse, it's a popular custom to walk across the street and dive into one of several family-style mountain cooking restaurants.

The noble Cherokees once reigned supreme over north Georgia's mountains, rivers, and forests, leaving behind a culinary heritage of corn bread, corn puddings, pumpkin pies, and roasted deer meat. These have melded with the southern appetite for barbecued pork, Brunswick stew, and fresh vegetables which seem to simmer for days before going on the dining tables of this lovely, historic region.

SOUTH GEORGIA: FROM PLAINS COUNTRY TO THE OKEFENOKEE

South Georgia remains an unhurried land of gracious living where the peanut and pecan reign supreme. Our state's leading agricultural products are supplied to cooks all over the world. But South Georgia cooks, naturally, have perfected the recipes for the most memorable pecan pies and pralines, peanut soup, peanut butter cookies, and scores of dishes given the zesty flavor of these sweet nuts.

Peanuts were first enjoyed by Spanish conquistadores in South America, who imported them back to Europe, whence they found their way to Colonial America. Pecans, on the other hand, were here all along and were a favorite delicacy of the native Indian tribes, who shared their secret with the first European settlers. The leafy green pecan trees flourish most abundantly in Georgia's far southwestern corner. Albany, a handsome, modern city founded by a Connecticut Yankee, hails itself as the "Paper Shell Pecan Capital of the World" in recognition of the millions of tons of this delectable nut that it processes every year.

The ante-bellum South of memories and magnolias lives on in the plantations around Thomasville. For one brief, shining moment, which lasted only from 1880 to 1910, this lovely town near the Florida border was the Camelot wealthy Northerners came south in winter to find. With its gentle climate, air fragrant with pines, and convenient situation at the southern terminus of the rail lines, Thomasville in that "golden age" was the Newport of its day. Its fame as a winter resort for the American aristocracy went south to Florida with the railroads in the early 1900s. But the magnificent plantations created by northern visitors can still be seen. And quail and pheasant are still prepared in the same marvelous ways by Thomasville's excellent cooks.

Columbus, south Georgia's largest city has also energetically preserved its heritage, which dates all the way back to the early 1800s when it was founded as a Chattahoochee River port. Although Coca-Cola is virtually synonymous with Atlanta, Dr. John Pemberton, who originated the formula, lived in Columbus, and his Victorian home is open to view.

In tranquil Stewart County is the recreated 1850s village of Westville, where hostesses preside over white-columned mansions, blacksmiths forge tools and horseshoes, cobblers make boots, and cooks prepare hearty stews, roasted meats, and breads over an open hearth as their predecessors did during the days when Stewart County was crossed by stagecoach trails. Visitors who follow the well marked Stagecoach Trail through the county seat of Lumpkin will see more than twenty homes built before 1850, as well as the Bedingfield Inn, a favorite stopping place for weary coach passengers and famous in its day for its comfortable beds and delicious hearth-cooked foods.

When President Franklin Delano Roosevelt created his Little White House near the town of Warm Springs, he became fast friends with Cason Callaway, who in the 1950s began creating one of the South's most beautiful resorts. Callaway Gardens at Pine Mountain now attracts visitors from all over, who come to swim, play golf and tennis, walk around the gardens and lakeshores, and savor the Gardens' famed muscadine preserves, smoked country ham, breads, and vegetables grown in the famous "Mr. Cason's Vegetable Garden."

Lake Seminole and Walter F. George Reservoir on the Chattahoochee are among Georgia's most productive fishing grounds, and cafes in Ft. Gaines, Blakely, Albany, Donalsonville, and Bainbridge are known for the glories of their catfish, bass, bream, and hushpuppies. And how happy are the tourists who venture off I-75 and find their way into cheerful emporiums of down-home southern cooking, where the menus are a catalog of favorites: fresh pole beans, sweet potato souffle, buttered corn bread dressing, catfish, mullet, and juicy apple and peach cobblers. Try over towards the Okefenokee Swamp too, where the legendary Suwanee River is born, another fisherman's paradise. It's what South Georgia's all about.

This is Georgia and dining in Georgia. We wish you enjoyment as you venture through these recipes and savor a flavor of the old as well as the new South.

William Schemmel
Dining/Travel Editor,
Atlanta Magazine

GRASSHOPPER PIE
The Boulevard Restaurant
Page 160

COLD CHERRY SOUP
Maison Gourmet
Page 50

RAISIN CREAM CHEESE STRUDEL
Dailey's
Page 164

SAVANNAH FISH STEW
Savannah Fish Company
Page 139

PENROD'S STEAK SOUP
Penrod's
Page 52

ORIENTAL PORK SPARE RIB
International Food Works
Page 76

COLD AVOCADO BISQUE
The Cloister
Page 42

CARROT SOUFFLE
Plantation Room
Page 151

BREAST OF CHICKEN VICTORIA
Seasons The Steak Club
Page 105

HOT FISH PATE
The Cloister
Page 29

HOMARD AU VEAU, SAUTE
Sea Palms Restaurant
Page 86

GINGER DUCKLING
Country Place at Colony Square
Page 96

GEKOCHTER SCHINKEN
Hofbrauhaus Inn
Page 73

FISH TERRINE
Michelle's
Page 128

BARBECUED SHRIMP
Joe Dale's Cajun House
Page 124

HIBACHI STEAK
Benihana of Tokyo
Page 64

MINCED BEEF AND EGG SOUP *(top photo)*
A Taste of China
Page 58

PEKING DUCK *(bottom photo)*
A Taste of China
Page 106

MARINATED CHICKEN LIVERS
The Pleasant Peasant
Page 34

SEAFOOD STRUDEL
The Delegal Room
Page 117

SOLE MONTEREY
Rusty Scupper
Page 137

BLANQUETTE DE VEAU
The Patio Restaurant
Page 84

SEAFOOD CHOWDER
International Food Works
Page 48

KAHLUA CHEESECAKE
The Public House
Page 177

TURNIP GREENS / CORN MUFFINS
Mary Mac's Tea Room
Page 150 and 154

SCALOPPINE DI VITELLO AL PESTO
La Grotta Ristorante Italiano
Page 78

GEORGIA SHRIMP GUMBO
St. Andrew's Restaurant
Page 138

THE DAYBREAKER
Daybreak Restaurant
Page 183

CHEF HEINZ SOWINSKI'S BOUILLABAISSE
The Brass Key
Page 40

CHOCOLATE DIABLO
The Peasant Uptown
Page 173

BREAST OF DUCK
Michelle's
Page 101

BRANDIED PUMPKIN CHEESECAKE
Carbo's Cafe
Page 162

NIGIRI—SUSHI
Benihana of Tokyo
Page 26

SHRIMP PIERRE RADISSON
The Boulevard Restaurant
Page 111

TROUT PONTCHARTRAIN
Jim White's Half Shell
Page 123

TORTE AU FROMAGE BLANC
International Food Works
Page 167

MONGOLIAN BEEF
The Sundial Restaurant
Page 87

LE MEDAILLON DE VEAU AUX ENDIVES
Nikolai's Roof
Page 83

23

CREME BRULEE
Plantation Room
Page 175

CASSEROLE MEDITERRANE
The Pavilion Dining Room
Page 131

CHOCOLATE MOUSSE
Michelle's
Page 172

LAS TRES SONRRISAS
Bentley's
Page 65

GRILLED SALMON STEAK
Winfield's
Page 145

CHICKEN AND DUMPLINGS
Davis Brothers Cafeteria
Page 97

ROAST RACK OF LAMB
Jonathan's Penthouse
Page 77

APPETIZERS

BENIHANA OF TOKYO

Peachtree Center, Ivy Mall Entrance, 229 Peachtree St. NE, Atlanta, GA 30303; (404) 522-9627.

Situated in a quiet corner of bustling Peachtree Center, downtown Atlanta's Benihana of Tokyo is actually two restaurants combined. In one large, authentically decorated dining area, patrons may enjoy Benihana's world-famous teppanyaki hot-grill cooking, with shrimp, steak, and chicken entrees prepared by specially trained Japanese chefs. Benihana also boasts downtown Atlanta's only sushi/sashimi bar, featuring rare delicacies from the sea prepared in a special Japanese way.

NIGIRI-SUSHI *(Basic rice and fresh fish sushi)*

2 cups of regular rice
3 cups water
3 tablespoons vinegar
1 teaspoon salt
1 tablespoon soy sauce
1 tablespoon sake or sherry
1 ounce wasabi (See Note), grated
   fine or fine horseradish
12 ounces fresh tuna, chilled or
   fresh salmon, shrimp, abalone,
   or red snapper
Garnish: pickled ginger,
   horseradish, and soy sauce

Place rice in a heavy saucepan, add water, set over high heat, and bring to a rolling boil. Cover, lower heat, and cook for 20 minutes. Then let stand in covered pan while preparing sauce. When ready to use drain any remaining liquid. In a small pan combine vinegar, salt, soy sauce, sake (or sherry). Heat to simmering. Remove from heat and stir into rice, blending thoroughly. Transfer the rice mixture to a large platter and let cool.

When cool enough to work with, mold into an oblong ball in the palm of the left hand. Place a pinch of wasabi or horseradish on top of each ball.

Slice the chilled raw tuna (or whatever fish you are using) into thin pieces, sized to fit over the rice balls. Arrange over the rice.

Refrigerate until completely cooled. Serve on large platter or lacquered tray, with pickled ginger, horseradish, and soy sauce.

Note: Wasabi available at oriental food stores.
MAKES 2 SERVINGS
Photograph, Page 22

THE BUGATTI RESTAURANT

Omni International Hotel, One Omni International, Atlanta, GA 30335; (404) 659-0000.

There are Sunday brunches, then there is the Bugatti *Italian* Sunday brunch, in a league all by itself. On huge banquet tables is spread an incomparable feast in this award-winning, four-star restaurant. Guests begin with fresh melons and strawberries, move onto cheeses, fresh-baked Italian breads, antipasto delicacies, and entrees that include veal, chicken, pasta, and seafood creations. Finally, with rich, steaming cups of espresso, the grand finale is the dessert table, laden with cakes, pies, and tarts.

PAGLIA E FIENO CON PESTO E SUGO *(Green and white noodles)*

8 ounces white linguine pasta, uncooked
8 ounces green linguine pasta, uncooked
$^{1}/_{2}$ cup butter, softened
8 leaves fresh sweet basil
1 teaspoon pine nuts
1 teaspoon walnuts
1 teaspoon Parmesan cheese
1 clove garlic, chopped
$^{1}/_{2}$ teaspoon parsley, chopped
Salt and pepper to taste
2 cups tomato sauce
   (see Basic Sauces)
$^{1}/_{2}$ cup Parmesan cheese, grated
Garnish: grated Parmesan cheese
   and parsley

In large saucepan bring salted water to boil.
Cook fresh pasta for 3 to 5 minutes for al dente, longer if desired. Drain off water using a colander.
For pesto butter, in a bowl combine butter, basil, pine nuts, walnuts, 1 teaspoon Parmesan cheese, garlic, and parsley. Season with salt and pepper to taste.
In a separate saucepan mix pesto butter and tomato sauce, bring to a boil, and reduce to a simmer.
Add pasta to the hot sauce. Add remaining Parmesan cheese and toss.
Serve with a garnish of Parmesan cheese and chopped parsley.
MAKES 6 SERVINGS

CLOCK OF 5'S

Hyatt Regency Atlanta Hotel, 265 Peachtree St. NE, Atlanta, GA 30303; (404) 577-1234.

Time flies when you are experiencing an outstanding lunch or dinner at the Hyatt Regency's beautiful Clock of 5's Restaurant. In an atmosphere of brass and copper and filled with antique and reproduction clocks of all shapes and sizes, all set at 5 o'clock, you will enjoy sumptuous five-course prix-fixe dinners and service that is cheerful and helpful. You may also enjoy your favorite cocktails and wines.

POPCORN SHRIMP WITH ZUCCHINI

*2 large zucchini, washed and
    quartered lengthwise*
*1 small package tempura batter
    (see Note)*
2 large onions, sliced
*2 potato skins, already baked
    (see Polaris recipe for Potato
    Skins, page 35)*
*1 pound bay shrimp (about
    40 count)*
*Flour seasoned with salt, pepper,
    cayenne, paprika*
Garnish: parsley and lemon

Remove ends of zucchini and cut into quarters lengthwise. Flour and dip into tempura batter and deep fry until golden brown. Slice onions, flour, and deep fry until golden brown also. Then deep fry potato skins until golden brown. Place zucchini, onion, and potato skins in a warm oven set at 200 degrees F.

Flour shrimp with seasoned flour and quickly deep fry.

Take an oblong wicker basket and line with cloth napkins. Arrange onions in bottom of basket, then place zucchini along sides facing outward and potato skins along other side. Place shrimp in center

Serve with lemon and chopped parsley. A nice tossed green salad could be served with this dish. Use as appetizer, lunch, or entire light meal.

*Note: Tempura batter available from oriental
food stores and in gourmet food section of
grocery stores.*
MAKES 4 SERVINGS

THE CLOISTER

Sea Island, GA 31561; (912) 638-3611.

Like a czarist grand duchess, The Cloister has reigned over the Georgia low country since its opening in 1928. Through the years, kings and commoners have come to appreciate The Cloister's Beach Club, Sea Island Golf Course, tennis courts, and the unmatched luxury of its cottage, villa and hotel accommodations. They keep coming back, as well, for the dining, which ranges from American/continental dishes, to barbecue and other southern favorites served at the famous Friday night Plantation Suppers on the beach.

HOT FISH PATE

*1 pound filleted sole or flounder or
    combination of sole, flounder,
    salmon, dolphin, king fish, or
    any size raw shrimp, peeled and
    deveined
Lemon juice, salt, Worcestershire
    sauce
2 medium onions, sliced, sauted
    in butter until limp
2 hard-cooked eggs, sliced
4 ounces fresh mushrooms,
    sliced, sauted in butter
4 tablespoons fresh chopped
    parsley
2 cups cooked regular rice
1 tablespoon milk
1 sheet puff pastry (see Glossary)
Salt and white pepper to taste
Clarified butter*

Marinate seafood in lemon juice, salt, and Worcestershire sauce for a minimum of 1 hour. Prepare onions, eggs, mushrooms, parsley, and rice. Spread out puff pastry sheet.

Place ingredients in layers, seasoning with salt and pepper to taste. Use moist ingredients first — onions, eggs, mushrooms, seafood, parsley, and rice last to soak up moisture.

Fold over sides to overlap. Carefully turn over and place on greased baking sheet. Reshape if necessary.

Make quarter-inch slits on top of pate at 2-to 3-inch intervals to permit steam to escape. Brush on milk for healthy browning while baking. Bake at 450 degrees F. for 5 minutes then lower to 350 degrees F. and bake for about 40 minutes more. Test with needle to see if done. Pâté should rest for 5 minutes before slicing. Pâté is improved by pouring in some clarified butter through the steam holes (use cream pitcher).

Note: Pâtés can also be made with brioche dough, or good pie dough. It can also be baked in an appropriate mold (Pullman loaf).

MAKES 4 SERVINGS
Photograph, Page 18

THE COLONY ROOM

Holiday Inn — Marietta, I-75 North at Delk Rd., Marietta, GA 30067; (404) 952-8161.

The Holiday Inn Marietta is conveniently located on I-75 North in Cobb County, a short drive from Cumberland Mall, the Atlanta Galleria complex, the Lockheed-Georgia Company, and downtown Marietta. Guests appreciate the tastefully decorated rooms, and enjoy such amenities as a large swimming pool, and banquet and meeting facilities. When it's time for dining and entertainment, the Inn's Colony Room is a pleasant place for breakfast, luncheon, and dinner, accompanied by wines and cocktails.

TURKEY SESAME

4 eggs
1 quart buttermilk
12 cups all-purpose flour
1 tablespoon coarsely ground
    black pepper
2 tablespoons salt
1 pound sesame seeds
1 raw turkey breast

Combine eggs and buttermilk in a mixing bowl and set aside. In a separate mixing bowl, combine flour, black pepper, salt, and sesame seeds.

Skin turkey breast; remove meat, and cut into 1-inch cubes.

Soak the turkey cubes in egg and buttermilk mixture for about 1 hour. Then mix the wet cubes in the flour mixture and fry in a deep fryer at 350 degrees F. until golden brown.

This fine tidbit snack can be enjoyed with your favorite dipping sauce, such as sweet and sour sauce, horseradish sauce, cocktail sauce, or French dressing.

MAKES 24 SERVINGS

THE MIDNIGHT SUN

225 Peachtree St. NW, Atlanta, GA 30303; (404) 577-5050.

Inspired by the breathtaking modern architecture of Denmark, The Midnight Sun is a dramatic showcase in the use of space and light created by world-renowned designer John Portman. The award-winning Scandinavian/European restaurant in downtown Atlanta's Peachtree Center surrounds a marble-tiered fountain atrium open to the sky. At night, lights beneath the fountain turn the marble to a translucent pink and gold. Soft lighting, fine linens, china, crystal, and fresh flowers heighten the romantic setting.

CEVICHE BAHIANO

²/₃ cup orange juice
¹/₃ cup lime juice
¹/₂ green pepper, cut into
*   1¹/₂-inch strips*
¹/₄ Bermuda onion, chopped
2 bay leaves
1 teaspoon salt
¹/₂ teaspoon white pepper
2 tablespoons fresh coriander
*   or parsley, chopped*
2 tablespoons white wine
1 pound small bay scallops or
*   sea scallops, sliced*
Garnish: lettuce (Boston lettuce
*   suggested) and pimiento*

Combine all ingredients for marinade in a glass or ceramic bowl. Add scallops.

Toss well, cover, and refrigerate overnight. Turn occasionally.

To serve, spoon mixture over lettuce and garnish with small pieces of shredded pimiento.

MAKES 6 SERVINGS

THE MIDNIGHT SUN

225 Peachtree St. NW, Atlanta, GA 30303; (404) 577-5050.

Great restaurants, like great wines, improve with age. After a decade and a half, The Midnight Sun, in Atlanta's dynamic Peachtree Center, continues to enhance its reputation as one of the city's most outstanding dining forums. The dinner menu has been expanded to embrace the finest of Scandinavia and continental Europe. The wine list contains many rare and costly vintages from the Christie, Heublein, and Napa Valley auctions, and is one of the largest in the Southeast.

ESCARGOTS EN CROUTE FIRENZE

1/4 cup butter
1/4 cup shallots, finely chopped
2 cloves garlic, finely chopped
3 cups fresh spinach, finely
*   chopped*
1 teaspoon nutmeg
2 tablespoons heavy cream
2 tablespoons white wine
2 tablespoons Pernod
18 large escargots or 24 small,
*   chopped bite-size*
2 to 3 sheets puff pastry
*   (see Glossary and Note)*
1 egg yolk, beaten
1 egg white, beaten
*   Bernaise sauce (see*
*   Basic Sauces)*

In a skillet melt the butter and saute shallots, garlic, and spinach. Add nutmeg, cream, wine, Pernod, and escargots.

Place puff pastry sheets on floured board and roll out to one-quarter inch thick. Cut into squares, 2^1/$_2$ by 2^1/$_2$ inches. Brush each square with egg yolk; let sink in, then brush with egg white.

Place a mound of escargot mixture in center of each square. Fold pastry over basket-style to seal. Brush outside with egg yolk and then egg white.

Bake at 350 to 375 degrees F. for 15 to 20 minutes, or until golden brown.

Serve with Bernaise sauce.

Note: Two sheets will make 4 servings; 3 sheets will make 6 servings.

THE PATIO RESTAURANT

3349 Piedmont Rd. NE, Atlanta, GA 30305; (404) 237-5878.

The Patio is a small, romantic hideaway where guests come to savor the most superb French cuisine and wines, returning again and again. The Patio is a very personal kind of place. The owner/chefs are always on hand, moving from the kitchen into the dining rooms to meet with their guests and guide them with their selections. Yearly visits to Europe keep them attuned with the freshest culinary ideas from Paris and other dining capitals.

CHICKEN LIVER PATE

3 tablespoons lightly salted butter
1 pound chicken livers
6 1/2 ounces bacon (about 6 slices)
1/3 cup thinly sliced carrots,
    peeled and cooked
1 cup finely chopped onions
5 tablespoons butter, softened
1/4 teaspoon black pepper
1/2 teaspoon, plus 2 large pinches,
    salt
2 1/2 tablespoons dry sherry
2 pinches cayenne pepper
2 1/2 teaspoons anchovy paste

In a saute pan melt 2 tablespoons butter and saute chicken livers until tender, leaving slightly pink in the centers.
Cook bacon until crisp, and drain.
Cook onions very slowly in 1 tablespoon butter until soft and sweet (about half an hour).
Place all ingredients in a food processor. Puree until well blended and smooth.
Pack into small ramekins and serve with small squares of warm, buttered toast as an hors d'oeuvre, or put in a larger dish to serve as an appetizer.
MAKES 8 SERVINGS

THE PLEASANT PEASANT

555 Peachtree St. NE, Atlanta, GA 30328; (404) 874-3223.

In the early seventies, two young Atlantans opened The Pleasant Peasant on the edge of downtown Atlanta and immediately began an exciting new era in local dining. The Peasant was the first Atlanta restaurant to blend a casually sophisticated ambiance — tiled floors, a pressed-tin ceiling, plants and antiques — with a continental menu and a relaxed air that welcomed jeans, tuxedos, sports clothes, and designer dresses with equally open arms. Since Day One crowds have been SRO.

MARINATED CHICKEN LIVERS

2 tablespoons cider vinegar
2 tablespoons lemon juice
1 teaspoon garlic salt
1/2 teaspoon white pepper
1/2 teaspoon dry mustard
1 cup vegetable oil
1/2 cup flour
1 1/2 teaspoons salt
1/2 teaspoon black pepper
2 pints (2 to 2 1/2 pounds)
   chicken livers
2 tablespoons oil, more if needed
2 medium green peppers,
   julienned
Garnish: leaf lettuce and 18
   cherry tomatoes

Prepare marinade by combining vinegar, lemon juice, garlic salt, white pepper, and mustard in a blender or food processor and blend for 30 seconds. Gradually add vegetable oil in a stream and blend until smooth. Refrigerate until needed.

Mix flour, salt, and pepper in a shallow pan. Dredge livers in flour. Heat 2 tablespoons oil in a skillet over medium heat. Saute livers a few at a time until firm but still pink. Remove from heat and put in a bowl. Add the peppers to livers. Pour dressing over and marinate several hours or overnight in refrigerator.

To serve place livers on leaf lettuce and garnish with 3 cherry tomatoes per serving.

MAKES 6 SERVINGS
Photograph, Page 20

POLARIS

Hyatt Regency Atlanta Hotel, 265 Peachtree St. NE, Atlanta, GA 30303; (404) 577-1234.

Step off the famous glass capsule elevators into the glowing blue dome. While you revolve leisurely above downtown Atlanta's busy streets, enjoy the grandeur of overstuffed chairs, love seats and sofas, in a garden setting of living trees in Polaris' new look. Sip an exotic specialty drink, and wines and the finest champagnes by the magnum or glass. Dining includes hors d'oeuvres, prime rib, hearty stuffed potato skins, and a rich assortment of pastries and other freshly baked desserts.

CHEF KLAUS MITTLEHAUSER'S POTATO SKINS

6 medium potatoes
1 ounce barbecue spice
1 ounce cayenne
1 ounce oregano
1 ounce thyme
$1/2$ ounce salt
$1/2$ ounce black pepper
$1/2$ ounce paprika
2 ounces garlic powder
18 slices bacon, minced
$1^1/2$ medium onions, peeled and
  minced
1 pound Cheddar cheese, grated
Garnish: chopped chives, sour
  cream

Slice ends off each potato. Cut potatoes into quarters. Cut skins off, leaving about quarter of an inch of potato on each. Place skins in salted water to prevent browning until all are peeled. Deep fat-fry at 360 degrees F. for 3 to 5 minutes or until crisp.

For topping combine barbecue spice, cayenne, oregano, thyme, salt, black pepper, paprika, and garlic powder.

Cook bacon until golden brown. Add onions and saute until limp. Add spices.

Divide equally on potato skins. Top with grated cheese.

Serve with sour cream and chives.

MAKES 6 SERVINGS

THEDA'S

1026¹/₂ North Highland Ave. NE, Atlanta, GA 30306; (404) 876-6616.

All around, there's an almost electrical buzz of conversation. Half the diners in this pleasantly contemporary restaurant seem to know the other half. A mainstay of the rejuvenated Virginia/Highland community in Atlanta's midtown, Theda's is a neighborhood gathering place, where friends come to enjoy superb continental dishes, great drinks, and friendly service. By evening's end, newcomers usually find that Theda's is their kind of place as well, and make plans for an encore appearance at the renowned Sunday brunch.

FRENCH ONION TART

1¹/₂ tablespoons dry yeast (1¹/₂ packages)
²/₃ cup warm milk
1 teaspoon flour
1 teaspoon sugar
3 eggs
2¹/₄ cups all-purpose flour, preferably unbleached
6 tablespoons butter, softened
1¹/₂ teaspoons salt
3 medium or 2 large onions, sliced lengthwise
¹/₂ cup sour cream
1 tablespoon poppy seeds
Salt and pepper

Combine yeast, half warm milk, flour, and sugar and let sit until foamy.

Mix yeast mixture with remaining milk, 1 egg, flour, 2 tablespoons butter, and salt. Knead for 5 to 10 minutes. Let rise at room temperature in a bowl for 1 hour. (Make filling in meantime.) When dough has risen, roll out on floured surface, then line a (10-inch) greased pie pan, with dough thickest at the edge. Set aside and let rise again. Melt remaining butter and saute onions until soft, not brown. Cool, then mix with 2 eggs, lightly beaten, sour cream, poppy seeds, and salt and pepper to taste. Fill pie pan.

Bake at 400 degrees F. for 20 to 30 minutes until bubbly. Serve hot.

MAKES 6 to 8 SERVINGS

20TH CENTURY RESTAURANT

Sheraton Century Hotel, Clairmont Rd., at I-85 North, 2000 Century Blvd. NE, Atlanta, GA 30345; (404) 325-0000.

The Sheraton Century Center, set within a beautifully landscaped office complex, is a favorite with business and pleasure travelers, offering lighted tennis courts and a heated swimming pool. The 20th Century Restaurant serves outstanding American and international cuisines, with dancing, and vivacious entertainment in the lounge that draws in local residents. For quiet relaxation, the Arcade Lounge offers an inviting ambiance of plush seating, subdued lighting, and your favorite libations.

COQUILLE A LA CENTURY

³/₄ cup butter
2 cups bread crumbs
1 pound (26 to 30 count) shrimp
³/₄ pound king crab meat
1¹/₂ pints cheese sauce

Cheese Sauce
4 ounces Gruyere cheese, grated
4 ounces sharp Cheddar, grated
2 ounces Parmesan cheese, grated
1 teaspoon salt
¹/₄ teaspoon white pepper
1¹/₂ pints whipping cream

Layer bottom of 6 individual casseroles with 2 tablespoons butter. Divide 1 cup bread crumbs equally between casseroles.

Add shrimp and crab meat and top each with cheese sauce. Add remaining bread crumbs and cook in 375-degree-F. oven for 12 minutes.

Cheese Sauce: Melt cheese in saucepan over low heat. Add seasoning and whipping cream, stirring until warm and smooth.

MAKES 6 SERVINGS

WINFIELD'S

100 Galleria Parkway, Atlanta, GA 30339; (404) 955-5300.

Winfield's, in the exciting Atlanta Galleria dining/shopping/office/hotel complex, adheres pleasingly to the successful Peasant policy of friendly service, a delightful atmosphere, great mixed drinks, and imaginative and always surprising American and continental cuisine. Portions are plentiful and attractively served. The high ceilings contribute to the wonderful sense of spaciousness; the striped awnings outside and the deep-green inside add up to its overall handsomeness.

GRILLED TUNA APPETIZERS

¹/₃ cup oil
2 teaspoons red wine vinegar
2 cloves garlic, crushed
1 teaspoon garlic salt
6 (4-ounce) tuna steaks,
* ¹/₂-inch thick*
1 tablespoon butter
8 ounces fresh mushrooms,
* sliced ¹/₈ inch*
2 ounces currants
¹/₂ teaspoon garlic powder
¹/₈ teaspoon white pepper
1 teaspoon parsley flakes
¹/₂ teaspoon salt, or to taste
Garnish: 6 lemon wheels and 6
* parsley sprigs*

Combine oil, vinegar, garlic, and salt.
Place tuna in container in 1 layer and cover with oil mixture. Marinate several hours or overnight. Heat butter until sizzling and very hot. Saute mushrooms, currants, and seasonings for 30 seconds, stirring to combine. Remove immediately.
Grill tuna over charcoal 30 to 60 seconds per side, until just opaque.
Place tuna in center of (9-inch) dinner plate. Spoon 1¹/₂ ounces of mushroom mixture across the center. Garnish each with lemon wheel and parsley sprig.
Note: The marinade may be used twice.
MAKES 6 SERVINGS

SOUPS · SALADS · SAUCES

THE BRASS KEY

2355 Peachtree Rd. NE, Atlanta, GA 30305; (404) 233-3202.

The Brass Key first opened in 1977, and has since become one of Atlanta's finest gourmet restaurants. In a candlelit Viennese decor, guests dine on luxuriant haute cuisine such as Chef Heinz' bouillabaisse, venison paella, jaegerschnitzel, and osso bucco. These splendid dishes are enhanced by the widest selection of French, German, Italian, and Californian wines. Luncheon is also a special occasion at The Brass Key. Delicious seafood, beef, and fowl entrees are accompanied by salads and hot and cold soups.

CHEF HEINZ SOWINSKI'S BOUILLABAISSE

1/2 cup olive oil
1 large onion, julienned
2 ribs of celery, julienned
1 medium fennel, julienned
1 medium carrot, julienned
8 large cloves garlic
1 teaspoon fennel seeds
1 teaspoon saffron
2 medium tomatoes, diced
4 cups Chablis
1 quart fish stock (see Basic Stocks)
1 teaspoon lobster base (see Note)
2 bay leaves
8 small, firm boiled potatoes, peeled
2 (1 1/2-pound) lobsters, split and cracked
12 fresh mussels
12 fresh little neck clams
12 ounces firm white fish (cod, halibut, swordfish), cut in (2-inch) thick pieces
12 large shrimps, peeled and deveined
8 ounces bay scallops
2 ounces Pernod (see Glossary)
1 tablespoon cracked pepper
1 tablespoon chopped parsley

In a heavy-bottom, 4-quart saucepan heat olive oil to moderate heat. Add all vegetables except potatoes. Add garlic, stir once, then cover. Steam for 4 minutes. Add fennel seeds and saffron, stir gently keeping vegetables firm. Add Chablis, fish stock, lobster base, and bay leaves. This is your basic stock. Adjust flavor with salt to taste.

Boil potatoes separately until firm but tender. In a large copper pan, or two smaller ones, layer in the seafood: lobster, mussels, and clams on the bottom, then fish, shrimp, and scallops on top to prevent overcooking.

Top everything with basic stock and cover. Over moderate heat, simmer for approximately 7 to 10 minutes. Check seafood for firmness.

Just before serving, splash with Pernod, and sprinkle with cracked pepper and parsley. Serve with garlic toast.

Note: Or use Knorr's Swiss Instant Fish Flavor Bouillon and Seasoning

MAKES 4 SERVINGS
Photograph, Page 21

BUCKET SHOP

Live Oak Center, 3475 Lenox Rd. NE, Atlanta, GA 30326; (404) 261-9244.

Transplanted from Underground Atlanta to a handsome location across from Lenox Square, the Bucket Shop is the place to meet brokers, bankers, and business people, and they still post the daily Dow Jones Averages. Along with juicy half-pound Bucket Burgers and cheeseburgers, the menu now also includes prime rib, lamb chops, and prime steaks, and excellent mixed drinks at the convivial 38-foot, polished mahogany bar, or at your table at luncheon or dinner.

OYSTER SOUP

24 fresh oysters
1 cup white wine
1 cup heavy cream
1 cup crushed saltines or oyster
*   crackers*
6 tablespoons butter
Pinch cayenne pepper

Open 24 fresh oysters, retaining oyster meat and liquid. Place oysters in saucepan and add wine. Bring to a boil, turn down heat, and skim liquid. Add cream, crushed crackers, and butter. Season with a pinch of cayenne pepper and pour into warm soup tureens. Serve with additional crackers on side.
MAKES 4 SERVINGS

THE CLOISTER

Sea Island, GA 31561; (912) 638-3611.

A resort that has earned the appellation "flawless" is The Cloister on Georgia's Sea Island. From its beautifully appointed dining rooms, to its tastefully modern guest rooms and world-famous Sea Island Golf Course, The Cloister runs with seemingly effortless ease. The dining is relaxed and elegant in a room that remains essentially the same since its beginning. Waiters quietly bustle around, making sure guests are always satisfied.

COLD AVOCADO BISQUE

*1 pint fresh chicken stock, cold
(see Basic Stocks)
2 small ripe avocados
1 cup sour cream
1 cup milk
Salt, pepper, and curry powder to
taste*

Puree all ingredients in blender. Chill and serve.

Note: Save the seeds from the avocados and add to the soup until serving time. This prevents discoloration.

MAKES 6 SERVINGS
Photograph, Page 17

CLOUDT'S

1937 Peachtree St. NE, Atlanta, GA 30309; (404) 355-7523.

Generations of Atlantans have relied on Cloudt's for the freshest fruits and produce, cheese, and gourmet specialty items. At midday, busy shoppers and business people take time out for a delicious lunch at Cloudt's. The attractive cafeteria-style menu includes the store's famous fried chicken, gourmet sandwiches, soups and salads, and a constantly changing selection of delicious hot entrees. Beer and wine are served, and diners enjoy their feast on the terrace or inside the store itself.

CLOUDT'S CHEDDAR CHEESE SOUP

$^1/_2$ cup butter
$^1/_2$ cup flour
4 cups chicken stock
  (see Basic Stocks)
2 medium carrots, peeled and
  finely chopped
2 stalks celery, finely chopped
1 small onion, finely chopped
4 cups milk
1 cup grated Cheddar cheese,
  medium to sharp
$^1/_4$ teaspoon baking soda
Salt and white pepper

Melt butter in a large saucepan, add flour, and stir to make a roux. (See Glossary).

In a separate pan heat the chicken stock and add the vegetables. Bring to a boil and cook until vegetables are tender. Add milk. Then add this to butter and flour and stir well. Mixture should cream immediately. Add cheese, baking soda, and seasonings. Taste and adjust seasonings.

MAKES 8 TO 10 SERVINGS

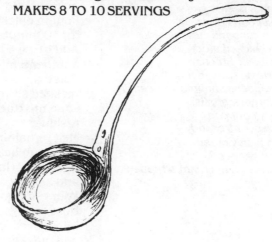

THE CYPRESS ROOM

Sheraton Atlanta Hotel, 590 West Peachtree St. NW, Atlanta, GA 30308; (404) 881-6000.

The Cypress Room presents superb American/continental cuisine, along with unmatched panoramic views of downtown Atlanta's booming skyline. Experience the mysterious sounds of the swamp in the aptly named Okefenokee Lounge. This midtown high-rise hotel is the essence of convenience. Downtown is a quick ride away on Atlanta's new rapid-rail system, and if you are driving, I-75 and I-85 are right at the hotel's doorstep. Guest rooms are large and tastefully decorated, with many unexpected luxuries.

SOUPE AUX ESCARGOTS

1/2 chicken breast, skinned and boned
1/2 cup each carrot, celery, chopped
3 1/2 cups beef bouillon
3 tablespoons butter
1/2 cup onion
1/2 cooking apple, peeled, cored, and sliced
1 banana, peeled and sliced
3 tablespoons flour
1 1/2 tablespoons curry powder
2 cups chicken stock (see Basic Stocks)
1 cup turtle soup, canned
2 tablespoons shallots, minced
12 escargots (snails), finely chopped
2 tablespoons brandy
1/4 cup heavy cream
Salt and pepper
Garnish: 3/4 cup cream, whipped

Poach chicken breast and chopped carrots and celery in 2 cups bouillon for 30 minutes. Remove breast, cool, and finely dice meat. Set meat aside.

Melt 2 tablespoons butter in a heavy pan over medium high heat. Saute onions until translucent. Add chopped apple and banana, sauteing briefly 1 or 2 minutes. Quickly sprinkle on flour and curry powder, stirring once or twice. Pour in chicken stock. Lower heat and simmer for 30 minutes, stirring occasionally.

Add turtle soup, diced chicken, and simmer another 5 minutes.

Puree the soup, then pass it through a fine meshed sieve, pressing down on the curried soup mixture with a spoon before discarding any residue.

Melt remaining butter and quickly saute shallots over high heat. Add escargots. Pour in brandy, ignite and flame. Add additional beef bouillon and heavy cream.

Pour escargot mixture into curried soup base. Heat soup, add salt and pepper to taste. Pour into 6 ovenproof cups, top with whipped cream and quickly brown under the broiler. Serve immediately.

MAKES 6 SERVINGS

THE FISH MARKET

Lenox Square, 3393 Peachtree Rd. NE, Atlanta, GA 30326; (404) 262-3165.

With its stylish pink-and-gray, turn-of-the-century decor, The Fish Market was a smash hit from the first day it opened in Lenox Square's new atrium. While the surroundings brought them in, this brainchild of the popular Pano's and Paul's has kept them coming. Fresh fish and shellfish are prepared with verve and imagination; seafoods are wrapped in a variety of pastries, and served simply broiled or sauteed. Drinks are excellent, and service is among Atlanta's most knowledgeable.

OYSTER VELOUTE *(Creamy Oyster Stew)*

6 tablespoons butter
4 tablespoons flour
$^1/_2$ pint oysters with liquid
2 cups bottled clam juice
$^1/_2$ cup half-and-half cream
Salt and white pepper to taste

Melt 3 tablespoons butter in a saucepan and blend in flour to make a roux. Cook gently 1 minute.

In another saucepan bring oysters to boil in clam juice and simmer 3 minutes. Remove oysters and keep warm.

Strain the hot liquid into the roux, blending well with a whisk. Bring to boil and simmer slowly for 3 to 4 minutes.

Add the cream and the remaining butter in small pieces. Season with salt and pepper.

Serve three oysters per cup.

MAKES 5 (6-OUNCE) SERVINGS

HALPERNS'

Lenox Square, 3393 Peachtree Rd., NE, Atlanta, GA 30326; (404) 231-5050.

Halperns' Seafood Bar and Gourmet Grocery in the Market Place at Lenox Square provides a lavish choice for the most exacting diners or cooks. A yen for steamed mussels, New Zealand lobster tails, cherrystone clams, seasoned shrimp, fresh stone crabs, or perhaps grilled swordfish steaks, along with your choice of wines and cocktails will be easily satisfied at our seafood bar and restaurant. While at the grocery, in addition to sea-fare, shoppers may purchase prime dry-aged meats, deli specialties, imported cheese, smoked fish, and fresh caviar.

HALPERNS' LOST-AT-SEA CHOWDER

2 to 3 tablespoons olive oil
3 tablespoons butter
2 green peppers, diced
1 cup celery, chopped
5 strips bacon, sliced
1 large onion, diced
4 tomatoes, peeled and chopped
3 large potatoes, diced in
   sixteenths
3 pounds assorted fresh fish,
   cut up
1 teaspoon white pepper
2 tablespoons basil
1 teaspoon garlic salt
1 teaspoon Worcestershire sauce
1 quart fish stock (see Basic
   Stocks) or bouillon
Salt and pepper to taste

Heat oil and butter in a pot over medium heat. Add green peppers, chopped celery, bacon, and onions; saute until onion is translucent. Add tomatoes and potatoes, and cook 10 to 20 minutes. Add fish, pepper, basil, garlic salt, Worcestershire sauce, and fish stock. Reduce heat and simmer 20 minutes more. Add salt and pepper to taste.

MAKES 12 SERVINGS

HUGO'S

Hyatt Regency Atlanta Hotel, 265 Peachtree St. NE, Atlanta, GA 30303; (404) 577-1234.

A harpist plays romantic airs. Tables gleam with fine silverware, copper serving dishes, crystal and china place settings. In this beautiful green and gray dining room, candlelight flickers on every table, and one of Atlanta's most knowledgeable serving staffs guides you through an evening of classical French cuisine. Entrees are draped in rich sauces; desserts prepared in Hugo's own patisserie are as sublime as you'd find in Paris itself. All together, an evening you and your special companion will long remember.

CHEF KLAUS MITTLEHAUSER'S LOBSTER BISQUE

2 lobster bodies (see Note)
1 cup butter
1 cup brandy
5 ounces mirepoix (carrots, onions, leeks, celery) (see directions and Glossary)
1/2 cup tomato paste
1/2 cup flour
Salt and pepper
1/2 ounce cayenne pepper
2 bay leaves
2 cups plus 2 tablespoons chicken stock (see Basic Stocks)
2 cups white wine
Garnish: 1/4 cup heavy cream, whipped; and brandy

Wash lobster bodies.

Heat butter in a pot suitable for the oven. Add lobster and cook for 3 minutes. Add warmed brandy and flame. Remove bodies and crush with side of a large knife or hammer. Put bodies aside.

To make mirepoix, chop vegetables roughly with skins on. Add to butter and cook slowly over low heat. Then add crushed lobster bodies, tomato paste, and flour and cook 5 to 7 minutes to brown.

Add seasonings, bay leaves, chicken stock, and wine. Whip until smooth consistency. Place pot in oven and cook at 250 degrees F. for 1 hour. Remove from oven and correct seasoning. Strain and serve with dab of cream and brandy on top of each soup dish.

Note: For lobster bodies, remove tails and big claws. Clean lobsters but leave tomalley (see Glossary).

MAKES 10 SERVINGS

INTERNATIONAL FOOD WORKS

Georgia-Pacific Center, 133 Peachtree St, NE, Atlanta, GA 30303; (404) 529-9416.

The International Food Works offers one of the most delicious dilemmas in town. Shall we have shrimp foo young at Chow's, tacos at Garcia's, a pastrami sandwich from The Deli, seafoods from On Ice, or a hamburger from Bailey's Broiler, and top it all off with pastries from Just Sweets? This colorful self-service restaurant in the Georgia-Pacific Center invites luncheon guests to sample all these culinary specialties in a friendly, cheerful atmosphere.

SEAFOOD CHOWDER

1/4 pound bacon
1 small leek, diced
1 small onion, diced
6 ounces potatoes, cut to
    1/2-inch cubes
6 ounces grouper (or other fish)
3 ounces bay shrimp, peeled
    and deveined
3 ounces diced clams
12 mussels
3 quarts fish stock (see Basic
    Stocks) or fish bouillon
Worcestershire sauce to taste
Salt and pepper to taste
1 pint heavy cream

Dice raw bacon and saute until half cooked. Add diced onions, leeks, and potatoes. Stir constantly, adding all seafood. Then add fish stock or bouillon. Cook until potatoes are tender. Season to taste with Worcestershire and salt and pepper. Add heavy cream last. Then serve.

MAKES ABOUT 10 SERVINGS
Photograph, Page 21

KOBENHAVN KAFE

Hyatt Regency Atlanta Hotel, 265 Peachtree St. NE, Atlanta, GA 30303; (404) 577-1234.

Imagine yourself in a sidewalk cafe, in the heart of Copenhagen's wonderful Tivoli Gardens. That's the feeling you'll experience while enjoying a delicious breakfast, luncheon or dinner, or after midnight snack in the Kobenhavn Kafe. You look across the exciting atrium lobby of the Hyatt Regency and watch a world of people swirl around you. Is that a famous film star sweeping past with her entourage? And she may be headed this way!

CHEF KLAUS MITTLEHAUSER'S LEEK, POTATO AND FRESH DILL SOUP

4 tablespoons butter
2 bay leaves
2 large Idaho potatoes, washed, peeled, and coarsely chopped
1 large carrot, washed, peeled, and coarsely chopped
1 large onion, peeled and coarsely chopped
2 heads of leek, thoroughly washed and coarsely chopped
3 pints chicken stock (see Basic Stocks)
Salt, pepper, fresh dill to taste
1 cup heavy cream
Garnish: fresh dill

Melt butter in heavy-bottomed pan. Add all vegetables, roughly chopped. Slowly cook until vegetables start to get tender. Add stock and bring to a boil. Add seasoning and dill. Cook for approximately 45 minutes over a low heat. Put through strainer, pressing as much of vegetables through as possible. Put back on stove and return to boiling. Add cream and correct seasoning to taste.

Serve piping hot with pat of butter on top with fresh chopped dill to garnish.

MAKES 4 SERVINGS

MAISON GOURMET

Broadview Plaza, 2581 Piedmont Rd. NE, Atlanta, GA 30324; (404) 231-8552.

Step out of Atlanta into a cozy cafe-pastry restaurant that could be in Paris or Amsterdam. Operated by a native of Holland, Maison Gourmet features fancy sandwiches, cheese platters, soups, extravagant pastries, and imported beers; a charming place for lunch or dinner before or after a night on the town. The Maison Gourmet offers the only Indonesian rice table, a feast of 12 exotic dishes, anywhere in Atlanta, plus teas, coffees, and other gourmet items that make lovely gifts.

COLD CHERRY SOUP

1 (16-ounce) can sour cherries
1 teaspoon cinnamon
Pinch cloves
$^1/_2$ cup cream sherry
1 pint sour cream
1 pint buttermilk
1 pint cherry Kefir (see Note)

Drain liquid from canned cherries, place in bowl, and add cinnamon, cloves, and sherry. Cover and let marinate for 2 hours.

Mix equal amounts of sour cream, buttermilk, and kefir. (Mix in advance for better consistency. Add to cherry mixture and chill for a couple of hours.

Note: Kefir is generally available from health food or gourmet stores or farmers markets in the dairy section. Cherry yogurt may be substituted.

MAKES 8 TO 10 SERVINGS
Photograph, Page 17

THE PAVILION

DeSoto Hilton Hotel, 15 West Liberty St., Savannah, GA 31401; (912) 232-9000.

On Madison Square, in the heart of historic old Savannah, the DeSoto Hilton combines the hospitality of the ante-bellum South with the conveniences and luxuries of today. The Pavilion dining room is likewise a charming blend of southern cuisine and congeniality with the cosmopolitan flavors of France and Italy. In this airy green and white dining room low country shrimp and she-crab soup share star billing with rack of lamb, medallions of veal, and Chateaubriand jardiniere.

SHE-CRAB SOUP

1 cup butter
2 cups flour
1 large onion, chopped
2 quarts fish stock
   (see Basic Stocks)
1 quart chicken stock
   (see Basic Stocks)
¹/₂ cup dry sherry
¹/₂ cup white wine
¹/₂ teaspoon salt
Ground white pepper to taste
¹/₂ teaspoon fish bouillon powder
   (see Note)
¹/₂ pound she crab (female crab
   and roe)
1 cup heavy cream
Garnish: lemon, paprika, and fresh
   parsley

In a large pan melt butter and blend in flour, cook until golden brown. Saute onions, combine with fish stock, sherry, wine and chicken stock, and add to flour and butter. Allow soup to simmer for 10 minutes, then strain into another pan. Add salt, pepper, fish bouillon, and crab meat and roe. Simmer for about 10 more minutes. Add cream and set aside.

Keep warm. To serve garnish each bowl with a slice of lemon decorated with paprika and fresh parsley.

Note: Use 1 cube Knorr's Swiss Instant Fish Flavor Bouillon & Seasoning.

She-Crab Soup was dedicated to George Washington in 1800 in Carolina and became famous along the Atlantic seaboard all the way up to New England. It has been one of the most requested soups ever since.

MAKES 10 SERVINGS

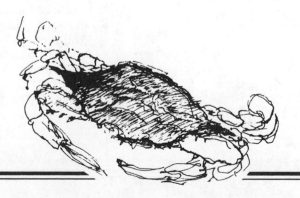

PENROD'S

2971-B Cobb Parkway, Atlanta, GA 30339; (404) 955-9599.

Penrod's is a gathering place, a meeting place, a place for brunch, a place for lunch and dinner, and a place to relax and unwind with friends. The lush interior has a feeling straight out of the classic film, *Casablanca* with tropical plants, stained-glass windows, and whirling ceiling fans. If Humphrey Bogart stepped up to a lady at the bar and said: "Here's looking at you, kid," hardly anyone at Penrod's would raise an eyebrow.

PENROD'S STEAK SOUP

1 quart onion soup (see below)
1 tablespoon Worcestershire sauce
1 1/2 teaspoons Kitchen Bouquet
1/3 cup cooking sherry
1 cup water
1 1/4 cups sour cream
1 tablespoon butter
1/2 pound sirloin tips, cubed
1 1/2 quarts water
2 tablespoons beef base
    (see Glossary)
10 ounces wide egg noodles
10 ounces Colby cheese

ONION SOUP
2 pounds onions, sliced 1/8-inch
    thick
1/2 cup butter
1 gallon water
1/2 cup plus 2 tablespoons beef
    base
1 1/2 teaspoons Kitchen Bouquet
1 teaspoon white pepper
1 1/2 teaspoons Worcestershire
    sauce

In a large pot on very low heat, place onion soup. Add Worcestershire sauce, Kitchen Bouquet, and cooking sherry.
In a mixing bowl, combine water and sour cream. Stir with wire whisk until thoroughly blended.
In a frying pan sautee meat in butter until well done.
In another large pot, bring 1 1/2 quarts water to rolling boil, add beef base and noodles. Stir noodles lightly so as not to break and cook until tender.
Add cooked meat to onion soup and stir.
Cool onion soup and meat to a warm temperature and add water and sour cream mixture.
Add cooked noodles and beef broth they were cooked in to soup.
Cook for 40 minutes at a low heat, stirring every ten minutes.
Slice Colby cheese into 10 (1-ounce) slices.
To serve, fill a (10-ounce) bowl with soup. Add 1 slice of cheese on top and melt under broiler.

Onion Soup
Saute onions in butter until golden. Drain.
In a large pot, place water, beef base, Kitchen Bouquet, white pepper, Worcestershire sauce, and bring to boil.
Add onions to stock and cook on medium heat 20 minutes.

MAKES 10 SERVINGS
Photograph, Page 17

PITTYPAT'S PORCH

25 International Boulevard NW, Atlanta, GA 30305; (404) 525-8228.

Just off downtown Atlanta's bustling Peachtree Street, Pittypat's moves to the slower, more congenial gait of the Old South of Scarlett and Rhett's day. Unwind from your hectic business or shopping day with a mint julep, an orange blossom, or your favorite libation in the Rocking Chair Lounge. Listen to some old-time melodies, then repair downstairs to the brick-walled dining rooms for a feast of traditional Southern cooking.

VEGETABLE SOUP

1 quart beef stock
   (see Basic Stocks)
2 stalks celery, sliced
2 pounds mixed fresh vegetables,
   including okra and others such
   as green peas, green beans,
   sliced carrots, chopped onions.
2 medium potatoes, peeled and
   diced
1/4 cup barley
1/2 cup tomato sauce
Dash paprika
Salt to taste
Bottled brown seasoning for
   soups and stews
Dash black pepper
Dash garlic powder

Put all ingredients into large pot, bring to boil, turn down heat, and simmer for at least 1 hour. Correct seasoning to taste.
As with most soups, this gets better with a little age on it!
MAKES 12 SERVINGS

QUARTERS COURT
RESTAURANT

Guest Quarters, 111 Perimeter Center West, Atlanta, GA 30346; (404) 396-6800.

At Guest Quarters, guests get a lot more than a room. They enjoy the spacious ambiance of one- and two-bedroom suites, with a richly decorated living room, dining area, and a kitchen equipped with virtually every conceivable gadget. For those who prefer to leave the cooking to someone else, there's 24-hour suite service and an attractive restaurant and lounge. Secretarial services, outdoor swimming pools, and convenience to Atlanta's finest dining, entertainment and business centers enhance Guest Quarters' acclaim.

HUNGARIAN CABBAGE SOUP

1 (5-pound) head cabbage, sliced
   or shredded
2 (16-ounce) cans diced tomatoes
   in sauce
1 (1-pound) box brown sugar
2 quarts strong beef or chicken
   stock (see Basic Stocks)
2 cups lemon juice
2 cups cooked roast beef, chopped
1 tablespoon dried basil
1 (6-ounce) can tomato paste
Garlic powder, salt, and pepper to
   taste
2 cups uncooked diced potatoes
Garnish: sour cream

Combine all ingredients, except potatoes and sour cream, in large pot. Bring to boil, and simmer for about 1 1/2 hours. Add potatoes and cook another 1/2 hour. Correct seasoning to taste.

Serve hot and garnish with sour cream.

MAKES 12 SERVINGS

RICH'S FOOD SERVICE

Georgia World Congress Center, 285 International Blvd. NW, Atlanta, GA 30313; (404) 656-7600.

Georgia is renowned for its superb food and hospitality. Enhancing this reputation is the Georgia World Congress Center, and its caterer, Rich's Food Service. The mammoth World Congress Center annually attracts hundreds of thousands of conventioneers and exhibitors. Operated by Atlanta's oldest retailers, the Food Service skillfully caters to small breakfasts as well as elaborate luncheons and dinners for several hundred. One of German-born Chef Gerd Giesecke's most popular creations is this Georgia Peach Soup.

CHEF GERD GIESECKE'S PEACH SOUP

10 ripe peaches
1 (6-ounce) can frozen orange
  juice concentrate
Juice and grated rind of 1 lemon
1 quart buttermilk
2 tablespoons honey, more or less
  according to taste
Pinch of salt
Pinch of nutmeg
¹/₄ cup cognac or Grand Marnier
Garnish: cinnamon and mint

Peel and slice peaches. Place in blender and add orange juice concentrate, lemon juice and rind. Blend to a chunky consistency and add remainder of ingredients. Let set overnight in refrigerator or chill for a minimum of 2 hours. Serve in bowls cradled in crushed ice with a dusting of cinammon and a sprig of mint for garnish.

MAKES 12 SERVINGS

SHALLOWFORD ROOM

Holiday Inn — Powers Ferry Rd. and I-285, Atlanta, GA 30339; (404) 955-1700.

This tastefully contemporary high-rise hotel is in the new tradition of Holiday Inns. On the northwest arm of Atlanta's 63-mile Perimeter Highway (I-285), it is a favored stop for business travelers and for shoppers at nearby regional malls. The Shallowford Room is popular with locals as well as hotel guests as are the beautifully appointed lounges offering live entertainment and extravagant "Happy Hours." Via I-285, many of metropolitan Atlanta's most exciting attractions are only a few minutes away.

CREAM OF OLIVE SOUP

1/3 cup melted butter
1/2 cup minced ripe olives
1/2 cup minced green
    pimiento-stuffed olives
1 tablespoon garlic, minced
3 cups medium white sauce made
    with chicken stock
    (see Glossary)
1 cup heavy cream
Salt and white pepper to taste

Put butter in saucepan over low heat, add minced olives and garlic. Then add heavy cream and bring to a boil.

Add white sauce made with chicken stock instead of milk, simmer for 15 minutes, stirring to be sure soup does not stick or burn. Add salt and white pepper to taste.

MAKES 4 SERVINGS

SPANKY'S

317 East River St., Savannah, GA 31401; (912) 236-3009.

Spanky's Pizza Galley and Saloon is a warm, personable landmark on Savannah's historic Riverfront Plaza. Surrounded by 250 years of Savannah's past, and with panoramic views of the mammoth ships moving through the busy harbor, Spanky's has become a favorite of Savannahians and visitors, who savor the delectable pizza and other treats in an atmosphere of mellow old brick and good fellowship. Spanky's friendly bar is also a popular stop for browsers and shoppers on the riverfront.

SPANKY'S HOMESTYLE CLAM CHOWDER

1 cup butter
1 pound chopped clams
2 medium-size potatoes, finely
   chopped
1 large bell pepper, finely chopped
1 medium-size onion, finely
   chopped
3 stalks celery, finely chopped
1 clove garlic, crushed
$^1/_4$ cup sherry
$^1/_2$ teaspoon salt
$^1/_4$ teaspoon black pepper
$^1/_4$ teaspoon cayenne pepper
2 cups water
4 tablespoons flour, sifted
$^1/_2$ cup half-and-half cream
Oyster crackers

In a saucepan, melt $^1/_2$ cup butter and saute clams, potatoes, bell pepper, onion, celery, garlic, and sherry for 15 minutes. Add salt, black pepper, cayenne pepper, and water. Bring to a rapid boil, and reduce heat to simmer and cook for 30 minutes.

In another saucepan melt the remaining butter and add flour gradually, stirring until smooth. Reduce heat under the clam chowder mixture further, and slowly add half-and-half while stirring constantly. Remove from heat and gradually stir in the butter and flour mixture until completely dissolved. Return to heat and stir until mixture thickens.

Serve piping hot with oyster crackers.

MAKES 6 SERVINGS

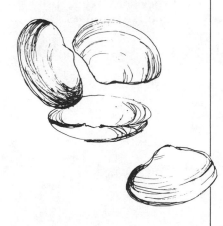

A TASTE OF CHINA

233 Peachtree St. NE, Atlanta, GA 30303; (404) 659-6333.

A Taste of China, one of Atlanta's most beautiful oriental restaurants, is like a grand culinary tour of one of the world's most exotic countries. Tucked away in a quiet corner of Peachtree Center, but definitely a reward for those who seek it out, the gourmet menu offers five provincial Chinese cuisines: Cantonese, Mandarin, Shanghai, Szechuan, and Wu-Xi. The restaurant will prepare any Chinese dish, even if not on the menu, upon request, if the ingredients are available.

MINCED BEEF AND EGG SOUP

$5^1/_2$ ounces ground beef
1 teaspoon salt
$4^1/_2$ teaspoons cornstarch
$^1/_4$ teaspoon baking soda
1 teaspoon soy sauce (light)
Water
3 egg whites
3 tablespoons oil
4 cups chicken stock
    (see Basic Stocks)
1 teaspoon monosodium
    glutamate
Dash of pepper
6 green onions, white part only,
    shredded

Mix beef with $^1/_2$ teaspoon salt, $1^1/_2$ teaspoons cornstarch, baking soda, soy sauce, and 2 tablespoons water, and marinate for 15 minutes. Beat egg whites until creamy. (Whites will become creamy if beaten with chopsticks in the Chinese manner.)

In a wok, bring 4 cups of water to a boil. Add beef mixture and cook rapidly, stirring continuously. Set beef aside.

Rinse wok. Heat oil and add chicken stock to the wok. When stock begins to boil return beef and season with remaining salt and monosodium glutamate.

Mix 3 teaspoons cornstarch and pepper with 6 teaspoons water. Add to beef soup and stir thoroughly.

Add beaten egg white and stir again.

Pour soup into serving bowl or tureen. Sprinkle with shredded green onions and serve.

MAKES 8 SERVINGS
Photograph, Page 19

TOULOUSE

Colony Square Hotel, Peachtree and 14th Sts., Atlanta, GA 30361; (404) 892-6000.

At Toulouse, it's the extra flourishes that turn a memorable evening into a masterpiece. Named for Atlanta's sister city in France, this garden-like restaurant in the Colony Square Hotel surrounds diners with unexpected luxuries. While savoring a five-course classical French dinner, guests enjoy chilled spring water, a table elegant with Wedgewood china, fine crystal, silver flatware, fresh flowers, and matches imprinted with their names in gold. The staff has been carefully selected to provide the most attentive and knowledgeable service.

CREME DUBARRY

1 large head of cauliflower
1 large onion
4 tablespoons butter
$^1/_3$ cup white wine
3 quarts chicken broth
   (see Basic Stocks)
Salt and pepper to taste
4 cups heavy cream

Clean and cut cauliflower into small pieces. Chop onion in large stockpot and saute in butter. Add cauliflower and wine to onions and simmer for 10 minutes.

Add chicken broth and simmer over low heat for 45 minutes. Season with salt and freshly ground white pepper.

Blend mixture in blender at medium speed. Return to stove and add cream. Heat to boiling point, turn down heat, and simmer until reduced to consistency of heavy (whipping) cream.

Adjust seasoning to taste.

Serve hot.

MAKES 8 SERVINGS

THE MAGNOLIA ROOM

Rich's Department Store, 45 Broad St. SW, Atlanta, GA 30303; (404) 586-5421.

The Magnolia Room has been synonymous with hospitality for generations of Atlanta shoppers and downtown business people. Guests pass through a pleasing reception area graced with Mexican tiles and brass rails, into a tastefully contemporary dining room of light orange and green. The innovative menu includes many American favorites and such pleasant surprises as quiche, souffles, barbecued ribs, shrimp, and a variety of pastas. You can enjoy a refreshing drink before heading back to the office or the rigors of shopping.

RICH'S CHICKEN SALAD AMANDINE *with Frozen Fruit Salad*

3 1/2 pounds chicken breasts
6 stalks celery, diced
2 tablespoons salt
1/2 tablespoon white pepper
2 cups mayonnaise
1/2 cup pickle relish
Garnish: 1/2 cup toasted almond
*   slices*

Frozen Fruit Salad
1 (8-ounce) package cream cheese
1/2 cup powdered sugar
1/3 cup mayonnaise
2 teaspoons vanilla extract
1 (61/2-ounce) can sliced peaches,
*   well drained*
1/2 cup maraschino cherry halves,
*   well drained*
1 (26-ounce) can fruit cocktail,
*   well drained*
1 (13-ounce) can crushed
*   pineapple, well drained*
2 cups miniature marshmallows
1/2 cup whipping cream, whipped
Few drops food coloring, if desired

To make Chicken Salad: Boil chicken breasts in lightly salted water until meat is tender. Reserve stock for future use. Let chicken cool. Separate meat from bones and skin by pulling. Leave chicken in medium-size strips.

Toss remaining ingredients, except almonds, with chicken meat. Cover and refrigerate until serving.

Garnish with almonds and serve with Frozen Fruit Salad.

Frozen Fruit Salad

Put cream cheese in mixer. Add powdered sugar and blend in mayonnaise. Add vanilla extract. Fold in fruit and marshmallows gently. Whip cream separately and gently fold into fruit mixture. Add food coloring if desired.

Ladle into large paper souffle cups or muffin liners. Freeze immediately. Defrost about 15 minutes before serving. Do not allow to get soft. Remove souffle cups or muffin liners before serving.

MAKES 12 SERVINGS

DAN JONES' EATING AND
DRINKING ESTABLISHMENT

1834 Midtown Dr., Columbus, GA 31906; (404) 568-3515.

This lively old English-style pub and restaurant features prime rib, steaks, seafoods, and salads in comfortable, relaxed surroundings. Columbusites flock here not only for excellent dining, but for nightly live entertainment and dancing. During the football season, the big-screen TV is a focal point of the spacious lounge. The family-owned restaurant is open for dinner Monday through Saturday and is also available for private breakfasts and luncheons.

HOT BACON DRESSING

*2 cups bacon fat (may use part
    salad oil)*
24 slices bacon
1 medium onion, very finely diced
1 cup brown sugar
2 cups apple cider vinegar
White pepper
Salt

In a skillet heat bacon fat. Saute bacon, remove from pan, and add diced onion to fat. Saute onion until transparent. Chop bacon and add bacon bits back to skillet along with sugar. Stir until sugar is dissolved.

Slowly whip in vinegar, pouring in a steady stream, until well mixed. Add pepper and salt to taste.

Keep dressing warm in a chafing dish.

Serve with fresh spinach leaves that have been washed and stemmed. Offer bowls of chopped eggs, sliced fresh mushrooms, and Parmesan cheese alongside.

MAKES ABOUT 5 CUPS

"A man is in general better pleased when he has had a good dinner upon his table, than when his wife talks in Greek."

SAMUEL JOHNSON

MEATS

BENIHANA OF TOKYO

2143 Peachtree Rd. NE, Atlanta, GA 30309; (404) 355-8565.

Step off of busy Peachtree Road into the serene oriental atmosphere that Benihana of Tokyo has brought to Atlanta. Much of this beautiful building was originally a farmhouse transported to Georgia from Japan. Paintings and other art objects are fine examples of Japanese handicraft. Guests sit around a steel hibachi grill while skilled chefs artfully prepare seasoned shrimp, steak, and chicken entrees, with an array of vegetables. Your evening is enhanced by a gracious serving staff in authentic costume.

HIBACHI STEAK

4 teaspoons soybean oil
1¹/₂ to 2 pounds boneless sirloin
   steak
8 to 10 large mushrooms, sliced
   vertically
Salt and pepper to taste

Heat nonstick skillet. (If using electric skillet, set at 350 degrees F.) Add oil to heated skillet.
Cut steak into bite-size cubes or slices, place in skillet with mushrooms and cook, tossing gently, until done to desired tenderness (add additional oil if necessary).
Season with salt and pepper to taste and serve hot.
MAKES 4 SERVINGS
Photograph, Page 18

BENTLEY'S

Atlanta Marriott Hotel-Airport, 4711 Best Rd., College Park, GA 30307; (404) 766-7900.

When is an airport restaurant an extraordinary experience? When it's Bentley's at the Atlanta Marriott Hotel-Airport. Tables in this pleasant, contemporary room are nestled among old books and vintage automobiles. Each evening the chef prepares a fresh seafood catch and lobster flown in live from New England. For beef-lovers, specialties include filet mignon or tenderloin paired with stuffed quail. Luncheon fare includes an appetizing buffet, sandwiches, salads, and special entrees.

LAS TRES SONRRISAS *(The Three Smiles)*

Lobster Sauce
1/2 cup butter
1 medium onion, coarsely
    chopped
1 carrot, coarsely chopped
1 rib of celery, coarsely chopped
1 clove of garlic, minced
Reserved remainders of
    lobster shell
3 bay leaves
Pinch of thyme
Salt and pepper to taste
1 1/2 tablespoons tomato paste
1 cup flour
1 quart fish stock (see
    Basic Stocks)
2 ounces dry white wine
Dash cognac
1/2 cup heavy cream

Las Tres Sonrrisas
2 tablespoons butter
1 pound tenderloin, cut into 24
    half-inch medallions
4 (8-ounce) live lobster tails, meat
    cut into 24 medallions
4 large cherry tomatoes
8 coquille shells
Selection of vegetables of choice
4 servings of saffron rice
Garnishes of choice

To make lobster sauce: in a saucepan, melt butter, add onion, carrot, celery, and garlic and brown lightly.

With a mallet, coarsely crush lobster shell and add to vegetables at a low heat, being careful not to burn butter. Add spices and simmer until reduced, about 40 minutes. Add tomato paste and mix well, and blend in flour to thicken. Stir in fish stock until mixture is creamy and comes to a boil. Simmer for 30 minutes, stirring constantly. Remove from heat and strain through cheesecloth.

Return to low heat. Add wine, cognac, and cream. Stir until smooth. Simmer for an additional 5 minutes and remove from heat.

Las Tres Sonrrisas

In a saute pan quickly sear tenderloin in 1 tablespoon butter.

In skillet in remaining butter, saute sliced lobster tails for one minute, turning once.

Trim end from tomatoes so they will lie flat. Cut each in half. Then lightly saute.

Cook saffron rice according to directions.

In one coquille shell arrange tomatoes around, place beef over tomatoes, then lobster over beef. Coat each layer with a teaspoonful of lobster sauce.

In another coquille shell, arrange a selection of vegetables and a mold of saffron rice.

Place both shells on a large dinner plate and garnish with such items as green lemon leaves, lemon basket, tomato rose, and sprig of parsley.

MAKES 4 SERVINGS

Photograph, Page 24

BROOKWOOD DINING ROOM

The Riviera Hotel, 1630 Peachtree St. NE, Atlanta, GA 30367; (404) 875-9711.

Since 1969, the Riviera has been a hallmark of hospitality on Atlanta's famous Peachtree Street. Enjoying a convenient location a few blocks from Colony Square and the Memorial Arts Center, halfway between downtown and the exciting Buckhead residential/commercial district, it's no wonder the Riviera is a favorite with out-of-town business travelers. The Brookwood Dining Room offers excellent American/continental cuisine, and fine entertainment is available within a few steps of the luxurious guest rooms.

LES MEDAILLONS DE BOEUF PERIGOURDINE

2 (6-ounce) filets beef
Salt and pepper
2 artichoke bottoms, canned
   (reserve liquid from can)
8 slices beef marrow (see Note)
5 tablespoons butter
2 (3-inch) rounds bread, cut from
   your favorite bread
¹/₂ cup Madeira wine
¹/₂ cup beef stock (see
   Basic Stocks)
2 tablespoons truffles, finely
   chopped (available from
   gourmet food stores)

Sprinkle filets with salt and pepper. Heat artichokes in reserved liquid from can and keep warm.

Poach marrow in simmering salt water for 3 minutes. Keep warm.

Saute bread rounds in 2 tablespoons butter until golden brown on both sides. Drain on absorbent paper.

Heat 1 tablespoon butter in skillet and saute filets over high heat for about 5 minutes on each side until well browned, but still rare. Transfer to warm serving dish, placing each filet on a round of sauted bread.

Pour off excess butter and fat in pan and add Madeira. Cook until wine is reduced by half. Add beef stock and truffles. Swirl in 2 tablespoons butter.

To serve, arrange an artichoke bottom on top of each filet, put 4 slices of poached marrow in each artichoke "cup" and spoon sauce over all.

Note: Ask your butcher to save marrow for you.
MAKES 2 SERVINGS

THE BUGATTI RESTAURANT

Omni International Hotel, One Omni International, Atlanta, GA 30335; (404) 659-0000.

Dining at The Bugatti is very much like a vicarious voyage on one of the majestic ocean liners of yore. Ensconced on plush green banquettes, tables laden with starched linens, fresh flowers, fine crystal and table settings, the tuxedoed serving corps presents a beguiling host of Northern Italian temptations: luscious pastas in cream sauces, veal in a dozen seductive ways, and for dessert, light frothy souffles set off by the aromatic richness of fresh espresso, and perhaps a glass of warmed Sambuca.

FILETTI DI VITELLO CON FUNGHI
(Medallions of white veal with mushrooms)

12 (3-ounce) veal tenderloins
Salt and pepper to taste
1 cup flour
$^1/_2$ cup butter
$^1/_4$ cup white wine
$^1/_2$ cup veal stock (see Basic
   Stocks and Note)
1 pound fresh mushrooms
$^1/_4$ cup butter
1 tablespoon fresh parsley,
   chopped

Season veal with salt and pepper. Dredge in flour. In saute pan melt half a cup butter until hot, and saute veal on both sides until brown. Remove from pan and keep warm.

Drain off butter. Add wine to pan and deglaze. Add veal stock to wine, bring to a boil, simmer until reduced by half.

In a separate skillet melt remaining butter and saute mushrooms. Add to sauce.

Top veal with sauce, and serve with chopped parsley.

Note: One teaspoon chicken base dissolved in half cup water may be substituted.

MAKES 6 SERVINGS

CLEO'S PEARL

3850 Roswell Rd. NE, Atlanta, GA 30342; (404) 261-7171.

When Julius Caesar first paid call on Egypt, the wily Cleopatra sought to seduce him with a feast of a hundred courses. Into Great Caesar's wine goblet was dropped a pearl of flawless perfection, symbolizing the honor of his presence. Diners at Cleo's Pearl will likely find no such baubles in their goblets, but the gracious staff at this sumptuous establishment does promise that every dish on their American and continental menu, and the wines, cocktails, and service will be a jewel long remembered.

RACK OF LAMB DIJONNAISE *with Fresh Mint Sauce*

1 (4-pound) split rack of domestic
  lamb
$^1/_4$ cup oil
$^1/_2$ teaspoon salt
$^1/_2$ teaspoon ground pepper
$^1/_4$ teaspoon rosemary
1 bunch fresh mint
$^1/_4$ cup red vinegar
$^1/_4$ cup water
Sugar to taste
Pepper to taste
$^1/_4$ cup Dijon mustard
2 tablespoons butter
6 tablespoons bread crumbs
1 clove garlic
$^1/_4$ teaspoon rosemary
1 teaspoon parsley, chopped

Have butcher scrape all fat from lamb and remove connective tissue from bones down to tenderloin. Brush with oil and rub in salt, pepper, and rosemary leaves. Let stand for a couple of hours.

To make mint sauce, finely chop fresh mint and mix with vinegar, water, sugar, salt, and pepper to taste.

Preheat oven to 450 degrees F. Cover lamb with foil and roast for 3 to 5 minutes. Baste with mustard and pan drippings. Reduce oven temperature to 325 degrees F. and cook for 5 to 7 minutes more for rare.

Saute bread crumbs in butter with mashed garlic, additional rosemary, and chopped parsley. Before serving, coat lamb with seasoned bread crumbs and brown under the broiler on all sides.

Slice rack of lamb just before serving. Serve with mint sauce on the side.

MAKES 2 SERVINGS

W. D. CROWLEY'S

Peachtree Mall, 3111 Manchester Rd., Columbus, GA 31904; (404) 324-3463.

Atlanta's popular Crowley's restaurants have come to Georgia's second-largest city with their successful formula of great food and drinks in a warm, congenial setting. In an ambiance of tongue-in-groove wood, antiques, brass, and green plants, the Columbus Crowley's serves an eclectic menu of hamburgers and gourmet sandwiches, steaks, lobster tails, and hearty soups. The bar is one of the city's most popular meeting places, and their Champagne Brunch draws SRO crowds on Saturdays and Sundays.

VEAL CORDON BLEU

4 (4-ounce) veal loin or rib-eye
4 (1-ounce) ham slices
8 slices Swiss cheese (³/₄ ounce
  per slice)
¹/₂ cup herb butter (softened
  butter, parsley, lemon juice)
Flour
Egg wash (see Glossary)
Bread crumbs

With meat hammer, pound each piece of veal until a thin, tender piece has been achieved. While pounding veal, keep a container of ice water on hand to dip meat hammer into, so as not to tear or break the veal.

Place pounded veal on a flat surface and top each with herb butter and 1 slice of cheese. Next, place ham slice on top of cheese and add remaining slice of cheese on top of ham. Spread remaining herb butter over cheese. Fold veal over and pat down to seal.

Coat veal in flour, dip in egg wash, then coat with bread crumbs. Place on lightly greased pan and bake in a 400-degree-F. pre-heated oven until golden brown, about 10 to 15 minutes.

MAKES 4 SERVINGS

GARDENTREE RESTAURANT

Terrace Garden Inn, 3405 Lenox Rd. NE, Atlanta, GA 30326; (404) 261-9250.

This dramatic, three-level dining room of the Gardentree Restaurant takes its name from a majestic, twelve-foot tree growing inside. The South Seas ambiance is enriched by a glass wall, looking out onto cascading waters. The Gardentree is famous for its Sunday Brunch Extravaganza, and its delicious breakfasts, luncheons, and dinners. The hotel is a big favorite with Lenox Square and Phipps Plaza shoppers.

KÖSTARD

*³/₄ pound puff pastry dough
  (see Glossary)
8 (1¹/₂-ounce) slices Swiss cheese
8 (1¹/₂-ounce) slices ham
2 pounds cooked broccoli spears,
  fresh or frozen
8 (1¹/₂-ounce) slices turkey
4 (4-ounce) slices Cheddar cheese
1 large egg, beaten*

Roll out puff pastry dough to 18 by 24 inches. Place in layers in the center of the puff pastry Swiss cheese, ham, broccoli spears, turkey, Cheddar cheese.
Brush the visible pastry with beaten egg. Fold the ends of the pastry over the ingredients toward the center, then fold the sides to the center in an envelope fashion.
Place on a greased sheet pan, folded side down. Brush pastry with remaining egg and bake at 425 degrees F. for 12 minutes or until golden brown.
Slice into 2-inch pieces and serve for brunch, lunch, or light supper.
MAKES 10 SERVINGS

GENE & GABE'S THE LODGE

936 Canton St., Roswell, GA 30075; (404) 993-7588.

Those who venture for the first time into the warm, cheerful rooms of The Lodge are invariably inspired to return again and again. Charmingly situated in historic Roswell's mid-19th-century Masonic Hall, The Lodge, like the original Gene & Gabe's in midtown Atlanta, rests its reputation on exquisitely prepared Northern Italian cuisine. The selection of pastas, veal, chicken, and seafood dishes reads like a symphony of this great cuisine, accentuated by fine wines and gracious service.

VEAL (OR CHICKEN) BOLOGNESE

6 veal cutlets (or 3 large boneless chicken breasts, split)
3 eggs
1/2 cup milk
2 tablespoons Parmesan cheese, grated
Salt and pepper to taste
4 to 5 cups bread crumbs
1 cup vegetable oil
6 slices ham, preferably Prosciutto
6 slices Mozzarella cheese
1/2 cup dry Marsala wine or dry sherry
1 cup chicken stock (see Basic Stocks)
Pinch oregano, parsley, salt and pepper
1/2 teaspoon lemon juice, if desired

Make wash of eggs and milk by beating them together. Season wash with cheese, salt, and pepper. (If using chicken breasts, pound them just enough to flatten.) Dip veal cutlets (or chicken) in egg wash, then into bread crumbs. Pat bread crumbs into veal cutlets (or chicken breasts) to prevent shrinkage.

Place oil in large skillet and saute veal for about 1 minute on each side (the chicken for 1 1/2 minutes on each side). Place in baking dish. Top each with slice of ham and a slice of Mozzarella. Pour off a little of the oil from skillet if necessary. Add to skillet Marsala or sherry, stock, oregano, parsley, salt, pepper, and lemon juice. Let simmer until it thickens slightly. Pour half of it over cutlets (or chicken), reserving rest to pour over finished dish.

Return meat to oven and bake at 350 degrees F. until cheese melts. Place on serving platter and top with reserved sauce.

MAKES 6 SERVINGS

GENERAL ASSEMBLY

Ramada Capitol Plaza Hotel, 450 Capitol Ave. SW, Atlanta, GA 30312; (404) 688-1900.

Whether the action's on the playing field at the adjacent Atlanta/Fulton County Stadium or in the legislative halls of the Georgia State Capitol, two blocks away, the most exciting "replays" take place in the lively restaurant and lounge of the Stadium Hotel. Ball players, legislators, sports fans, business and pleasure travelers, meet for cocktails and hors d' oeuvres in the Filibuster Lounge, and for luncheon and dinner in the General Assembly Restaurant.

MEDALLIONS OF VEAL AND LOBSTER

2 (6-ounce) lobster tails
Salt and pepper to taste
Paprika to dust lobster tails
6 tablespoons butter
5 medium mushrooms, finely
*   chopped*
1 small onion, finely chopped
1 small green pepper, julienned
4 (2-ounce) veal medallions
Pinch oregano
¹/₄ cup Marsala wine

Dust lobster tails with salt, pepper, and paprika. Saute in butter until almost done. Add mushrooms, onions, and green peppers and saute for about 3 minutes until tender. Add remaining ingredients, cover and simmer until veal is cooked, about 2 minutes.

MAKES 2 SERVINGS

HOFBRAUHAUS INN

1 North Main St., Helen, GA 30545; (404) 878-2248.

Overlooking the Chattahoochee River, on the outskirts of Georgia's Alpine Village of Helen, the Hofbrauhaus Inn might well be in the Alps of Germany. Lovely guestrooms overlook the Chattahoochee River and you may dine on a balcony that hangs over the river as well as in the charming dining room. This award-winning restaurant is noted for German and American dishes and boasts an excellent selection of German beer. Guests often entertain at the piano in the lively lounge.

GEKOCHTER SCHINKEN *(Smoked Ham)*

1 (10-to-12 pound) smoked
   country ham
Water
1 bottle dry sherry
1 bottle Moselle (white wine)
1¼ cups brown sugar
Bordelaise sauce, if desired (see
   Basic Sauces)

Soak ham in enough water to cover for 12 hours. Drain and cover with fresh warm water. Bring to a rapid boil, reduce heat, cover, and barely simmer for 2 hours. If the ham is to be served cool, simmer for a further hour. Then leave it to cool uncovered in broth.

If the ham is to be served hot, remove it from broth after 2 hours. Remove rind, notching it at the bone end to make a cuff, and trim off excess fat.

Put the ham in a roasting pan, add sherry and Moselle wine, and cover it closely with buttered brown paper. Bake at 325 degrees F. for 2 hours. Remove from oven and sprinkle with brown sugar. Increase heat to 350 degrees F. and roast until golden brown.

Serve the ham sliced thin in its own juice or, if you wish, accompany with Bordelaise sauce. At the Hofbrauhaus it is served with sauerkraut and German potato salad with a mug of beer.

Note: It is also good for breakfast with eggs.
MAKES 8 TO 10 SERVINGS
Photograph, Page 18

HUGO'S

Hyatt Regency Atlanta Hotel, Peachtree Ctr., 265 Peachtree St. NE, Atlanta, GA 30303; (404) 577-1234.

One of Atlanta's most acclaimed dining experiences, Hugo's is a gourmet restaurant of timeless elegance, recipient of countless awards, and a destination for Atlantans and visitors desiring an evening far removed from the mundane and ordinary. Hugo's European-trained chefs prepare classic French and continental dishes that are as beautiful to behold as they are glorious to the taste. Enriching your experience, a harpist plays romantic melodies, and Hugo's wine list offers an unparalleled selection of European and domestic vintages.

CHEF KLAUS MITTLEHAUSER'S VEAL *with Peppercorn Sauce*

8 (2-ounce) veal medallions from
    the loin
Flour to dust
Salt, pepper, paprika to taste
1 tablespoon oil
4 tablespoons butter
1 small can green peppercorns,
    crushed
4 tablespoons cognac
1 cup heavy cream
Garnish: fresh parsley

Pat veal until thin. Lightly flour and season with salt, pepper, and paprika. In a skillet heat oil and 2 tablespoons butter. Quickly saute veal until it loses its color (do not overcook as it will toughen). Remove from pan and pour off excess fat.

Add 1 tablespoon butter. Heat rapidly and then add green peppercorns. When hot add cognac and flame just until alcohol has burned off. Add cream and reduce. Add remaining butter. Pour over veal and garnish with chopped fresh parsley.

Serve with either saffron rice or vermicelli, with fresh basil and marjoram.

MAKES 4 SERVINGS

HUNAN RESTAURANT

6280 Roswell Rd. NE, Atlanta, GA 30328; (404) 252-8672.

Guests who venture into The Hunan are in for an exotic culinary odyssey to one of China's most picturesque regions. The cuisine of this mountain province is zesty and spicy, and nowhere in Atlanta are such delights as moshu pork, Hunan chicken, and Hunan crisp duck more deliciously prepared. All dishes are carefully prepared by The Hunan's renowned culinary expert, Frank Ma, and his especially trained team of chefs. A memorable experience for lunch and dinner.

FRANK MA'S TWICE COOKED PORK

*6 ounces boneless pork, trimmed
   of fat
1 slice of cabbage
2 pieces dry black mushroom
1/3 green pepper
1 clove garlic
1 green onion
4 teaspoons cooking oil
1 teaspoon soy sauce
1 teaspoon sugar
2 teaspoons hoisin sauce
   (see Note)
1 teaspoon monosodium
   glutamate
1 teaspoon hot pepper paste
Few drops sesame oil*

Slice pork, green pepper, and cabbage into inch-square pieces. Put in pot of boiling water and cook for 3 minutes. Drain. Soak mushroom in warm water for about 15 minutes. Slice garlic and cut green onion into inch-long pieces. Heat cooking oil in wok. Add garlic to hot oil and then immediately add soy sauce, sugar, hoisin sauce, monosodium glutamate, and hot pepper paste. Stir fry for a few seconds, and then add cooked pork and cabbage.

Add green onion to wok and cook for a further 2 minutes. Then drop in sesame oil.

Note: Available at specialty and oriental markets.

MAKES 4 SERVINGS

INTERNATIONAL FOOD WORKS

Georgia-Pacific Center, 133 Peachtree St. NE, Atlanta, GA 30303; (404) 529-9416.

The International Food Works was no doubt conceived to solve the dilemma of groups of people who can agree on almost everything except what they would like for lunch. In one large, busy, tastefully contemporary, self-service restaurant there is a choice of eight pavilions offering a dazzling variety of cuisines: from Mexican to Chinese, deli sandwiches to seafoods, burgers and hot dogs, to one that changes its repertoire every week.

ORIENTAL PORK SPARE RIB

4 pounds pork spare ribs
$1/2$ ounce fresh garlic, chopped
$1/4$ ounce fresh ginger, grated
6 tablespoons soy sauce
4 tablespoons hoisin sauce
    (see Note)
6 tablespoons oyster sauce
    (see Note)
4 tablespoons ketchup
6 tablespoons honey
2 tablespoons brown sugar

Saute garlic and ginger in small amount of fat. Add to this soy sauce, hoisin, oyster sauce, ketchup, honey, and brown sugar. Bring to a boil, cook for 5 minutes. Pour over spare ribs and cool. Let ribs sit in this marinade for 24 hours. Remove ribs from marinade.
Place ribs on rack and bake in oven at 350 degrees F. for about $1 1/2$ hours.
Strain marinade. Thicken by bringing to boil and reducing. Serve over ribs.

Note: Hoisin sauce and oyster sauce available at gourmet and oriental food stores.
MAKES 4 SERVINGS
Photograph, Page 17

JONATHAN'S PENTHOUSE

Merchandise Mart, 240 Peachtree St. NW, Atlanta, GA 30303; (404) 688-8650.

High atop the Atlanta Merchandise Mart, with Atlanta's million-and-one lights spread like a twinkling blanket beneath you, Jonathan's is like a lovely garden in the South of France. A fountain splashes around beds of seasonal flowers, music plays, and the service is discreet. Jonathan's cuisine is American and continental, and a pleasure at business luncheons or quiet suppers with someone special. Before or after dining, stroll around the open-air patio and watch Atlanta grow before your eyes.

ROAST RACK OF LAMB PERSILLE PROVENCAL

1 split rack of American lamb, chin bone removed, trimmed and Frenched with cap fat removed (ask butcher to do this)
3 tablespoons Dijon mustard
$^1/_2$ teaspoon salt
$^1/_2$ teaspoon white pepper
$1^1/_2$ teaspoons fresh rosemary
$1^1/_2$ teaspoons fresh thyme
2 teaspoons fresh minced garlic
2 tablespoons fresh parsley, chopped
$^1/_2$ cup dried bread crumbs
2 tablespoons olive oil
2 tablespoons butter, melted

Preheat broiler to 400 degrees F.

Place lamb on broiler pan, fat side up. Broil for 5 minutes, about 5 inches from the heat source. Turn lamb fat side down and broil an additional 5 minutes. Remove from oven.

Rub Dijon mustard into the surface of the lamb. In a bowl, combine the rest of the ingredients and mix well. Spread crumb mixture on top of lamb (fat side) and sides.

Bake at 350 degrees F. for 25 minutes for medium-rare.

Serve with Madeira sauce (see Glossary) or mint sauce.

MAKES 4 SERVINGS
Photograph, Page 24

LA GROTTA
RISTORANTE ITALIANO

2637 Peachtree Rd. NE, Atlanta, GA 30305; (404) 231-1368.

A gracious corner of Northern Italy on Atlanta's fashionable Peachtree Road, La Grotta consistently earns plaudits as one of the city's most outstanding dining experiences. Cuisine, service, and tasteful surroundings all come together to create something unforgettable in the courtyard setting. Entrees include creamy homemade pastas, seafoods, fowl, beef, and veal. For dessert, diners ascend to culinary heaven with zuppa Inglese (English trifle), zabaglione with champagne, and flaky cannolis rich with cream. The Italian wine list is an adventure in itself.

SCALOPPINE DI VITELLO AL PESTO

5 bunches fresh basil leaves
2 cloves garlic
4 tablespoons pine nuts, toasted
4 tablespoons imported Italian Parmesan, grated
$1/2$ cup olive oil
12 (4-ounce) scallopini (milk-fed veal) (see Note)
Butter
Oil
$1/4$ cup brown sauce or demi-glace (see Glossary)
Salt and pepper to taste

To make Pesto Paste, put basil, garlic, and half of the pine nuts in a mortar and pound with great patience, gradually adding the grated Parmesan until it is a delicious paste, and stir in the olive oil. Or you can use a blender which is quick and very effective.

Season the scallopini with salt and pepper, heat half oil and half butter in a skillet until hot and saute the scallopini for $1^1/2$ minutes on each side. Remove from the skillet and keep warm in a serving dish.

Drain oil and butter from the skillet and add pesto paste. Bring to the boil for one minute and add the brown sauce or demi-glace. Stir until it comes to a smooth sauce. Pour over the meat and sprinkle over the remaining pine nuts.

Note: Veal is the flesh of immature calves; it is white, clear, and soft, with little or no flavor since it comes from the very young milk-fed cow. This recipe should not be attempted without genuine milk-fed veal. Ask your butcher to scallopine the veal.

MAKES 6 SERVINGS
Photograph, Page 21

At the conclusion of a satisfying day on the business front, after a shopping tour where you have found just the right thing, when you are in the mood to enjoy quiet conversation with friends, or just to sit comfortably and watch the world go by, The Lobby Lounge in the beautiful Omni International Hotel is just what you've been looking for. The contemporary and elegant motif is enhanced by service from the personable staff. Hors d'oeuvres and drinks are prepared to perfection.

SZECHUAN PORK AND CHICKEN

1 (5- to 6-pound) pork loin roast, boned
Dry mustard
Thyme
1 cup plus 2 tablespoons sherry
1 cup plus 1 tablespoon Japanese soy sauce
6 cloves garlic, finely chopped
4 tablespoons fresh ginger, grated
12 pieces candied ginger, cut in slivers
10 (4-ounce) chicken breasts, skinned and boned
1/4 cup sesame oil
1/4 cup vegetable oil
1 (9-ounce) jar apple or currant jelly

Rub boned pork roast with dry mustard and thyme.

Make marinade of 1 cup sherry, 1 cup soy sauce, garlic, and ginger. Pour half over roast. Let pork marinate for about 24 hours. (Let stand all night in refrigerator and roast early in the morning, if you wish.)

Cut each chicken breast into 8 (1/2-ounce) strips. Pour remaining marinade over chicken and marinate for 2 hours. Drain. Heat sesame oil and vegetable oil in skillet and saute chicken strips over high heat. Drain in perforated pan. Chill.

Remove pork from marinade, drain, and place meat thermometer in thickest part of meat. Roast at 325 degrees F. allowing 20 minutes per pound. Baste with marinade. Pork is done when thermometer reads 175 degrees F.

Melt jelly in a heavy pan over medium heat. When it is bubbly add 1 tablespoon soy sauce and 2 tablespoons sherry. Let cook down for a few minutes, stirring constantly. Spoon over pork and cool in a chilly room.

Carve pork in 1/2-ounce strips.

Plating of chicken and pork.

Arrange the following on each plate: 2 Bok Choy leaves (as base), 6 (1/2-ounce) pork strips, 6 (1/2-ounce) chicken strips, 1 ounce snow peas, (cooked), 3/4 ounce bean sprouts, 1 green pepper, (seeded and sliced), 2 scallions, white end thinly sliced to resemble a "brush," 1 radish rose, 3 ounces Szechuan sauce (in side bowl) and 4 Bok Choy stalks, sliced on bias.

Note: This recipe can be used as an entree or an hors d'oeuvre.

MAKES 10 SERVINGS

LULUBELLE'S STEAK HOUSE

Atlanta Airport Hilton, 1031 Virginia Ave., Hapeville, GA 30354; (404) 767-0281.

Come into Lulubelle's and enter a plush atmosphere reminiscent of the turn of the century. Located in the Atlanta Airport Hilton Inn, only minutes from Hartsfield International Airport, Lulubelle's hearty American menu features succulent steaks, prime ribs, barbecued baby back ribs, chicken, chops, homemade soups, and a bountiful salad bar that accompanies every entree. Live entertainment and dancing are for your enjoyment nightly, in the lounge.

BARBECUED BABY BACK RIBS

3 gallons water
4 teaspoons salt
3 teaspoons black peppercorns
5 bay leaves
3 cups white vinegar
4 teaspoons monosodium
    glutamate
5 teaspoons pickling spice
6 to 8 pounds pork or beef baby
    ribs (have butcher cut to
    preferred size)

Bring water to a boil in a large pot, add seasonings, and then add meat. Simmer ribs for about 1 hour, or until tender. Drain. Place on baking sheet. Baste with Barbecue sauce (see below).
Bake ribs at 350 degrees F. for 10 minutes, turning ribs once. Remove from oven and serve with remaining sauce.

Chef's Special Barbecue Sauce
Mix 1 cup yellow mustard with $1^3/4$ cups ketchup. Add $1/4$ cup 57 Sauce, $1/4$ cup A-1 Sauce, 1 cup honey, 2 teaspoons white pepper, 2 teaspoons salt, 5 teaspoons sugar, 5 teaspoons lime juice, 3 teaspoons monosodium glutamate, 2 teaspoons chili powder, and $1/2$ cup liquid smoke. Mix well.
The sauce should not be cooked, but may be warmed over low heat. Do not boil.
MAKES 6 TO 8 SERVINGS

MARTEL'S

325 North Milledge Ave., Athens, GA 30601; (404) 353-8387.

In a charmingly restored southern colonial home, circa 1857, Martel's blends the hospitality of the ante-bellum South with the cosmopolitan cuisine of France and continental Europe. Guests seated in small, intimate dining rooms, each with a marble fireplace, have a choice of many outstanding dishes created from veal, seafoods, duck, and beef. Tableside flambee cooking adds an added dash of culinary magic to luncheon or dinner. Martel's wine list includes a large selection of French, German, Italian, and American vintages.

VEAL BEAUPRE

¹/₄ cup butter
¹/₂ pound boneless veal steak
6 fresh mushrooms, sliced
2 tablespoons shallots,
*   finely chopped*
6 tablespoons demi-glace
*   (see Glossary)*
2 tablespoons cream
2 tablespoons white wine
1 tablespoon cognac
2 tablespoons tomatoes, chopped
*   and seeded*
2 tablespoons parsley, chopped
Cooked rice

Pound veal and cut into small pieces. Brown butter in skillet and add veal. Cook for 2 minutes and turn over. Add mushrooms and shallots, and cook 3 minutes more. Add the demi-glace, cream, and wine. Stir. Add heated cognac and flame. Stir in tomatoes and parsley.
Serve over rice.
MAKES 2 SERVINGS

MAXIMILLIAN'S

1857 Airport Industrial Park Dr., Marietta, GA 30062; (404) 955-4286.

When it was built by a prominent Marietta attorney during the Great Depression, this charming country-style home was the first in Cobb County to be lighted by electricity. Today, guests at Maximillian's return to another era as they dine by the warm glow of candlelight and the hospitality of a roaring hearth. Yet the cuisine at Maximillian's is as contemporary and sophisticated as today, featuring a lovely selection of American and continental dishes, fine wines, and cocktails.

VEAL BENJAMIN

Orange-flavored Hollandaise Sauce
    (see Note)
4 egg yolks, room temperature
Dash cayenne pepper
¹/₄ teaspoon dry chicken stock
    or bouillon
1 teaspoon water
2 cups butter, melted
Juice of a freshly squeezed lemon,
    room temperature
Juice of a freshly squeezed orange,
    room temperature

Veal Benjamin
2 ripe avocados
Lemon juice and chopped parsley
    for marinade
2 pounds milk-fed tenderloin
    veal filet
6 eggs
¹/₄ cup half-and-half
2¹/₂ cups flour
2 cups butter
1 cup margarine
Juice of 1¹/₂ ripe lemons
20 ounces king crab meat
¹/₂ teaspoon salt
Dash white pepper
Garnish: kiwi fruit, red grapes,
    fresh parsley

To make Hollandaise Sauce: In a double-boiler, bring water to boil in lower pan. Take off heat, place egg yolks, cayenne pepper, and chicken stock in upper pan and mix with a whisk. Return to heat and continue to whisk until warm. Very slowly add melted butter, waiting for sauce to thicken before adding more. After adding 1 cup of butter, squeeze juice of ¹/₂ lemon into sauce. Continue to whisk, not allowing pan to get too hot. Must be warm only. Add remaining butter gradually, and remaining lemon. Then add juice from orange gradually.

To make veal: Slice avocado. Coat with lemon juice then parsley and keep at room temperature. Gently pound veal. Beat eggs and beat in cream. Dip veal in egg and cream mixture, and lightly coat with flour.
Melt butter and margarine in skillet and gently saute veal, sprinkled with lemon juice, until light golden color on each side.
Remove veal from skillet, dry excess butter from veal on a clean dry towel, and keep warm.
Place crab meat in same pan and heat for 2 minutes. Add salt and white pepper to taste. Drain crab on a clean dry towel.
To serve place veal on plate, top with crab meat, and decorate with avocado slices. Garnish plate with kiwi fruit, red grapes and sprinkle of fresh parsley. Just before serving top veal with orange-flavored Hollandaise sauce.

Note: If short on time substitute Knorr packet Hollandaise sauce mix and add orange for orange-flavored Hollandaise.
MAKES 8 SERVINGS

NIKOLAI'S ROOF

The Atlanta Hilton & Towers, Courtland & Harris Sts. NE, Atlanta, GA 30303; (404) 659-2000.

When is dinner worth a prolonged wait? When it is at Nikolai's Roof, the nationally honored Franco/Czarist aerie that crowns the Atlanta Hilton, whose awards include the prestigious Ivy Award for 1982. An enchanted evening begins with chilled Russian vodka aperitifs. Appetizers are highlighted by pirozhkis, meat-filled turnovers that could have made even the irascible Rasputin smile, followed by an array of entrees that include meats draped in sauces as rich as ermine, all served by waiters in Cossack costume. Elegantly appointed tables are well spaced for quiet conversation.

LE MEDAILLON DE VEAU AUX ENDIVES

8 (3-ounce) veal medaillons, cut
    from the loin section, free from
    all fat (ask the butcher to do
    this)—less expensive cuts may
    be substituted
4 tablespoons clarified butter
    (see Glossary)
1 cup flour
2 tablespoons shallots,
    finely chopped
1 cup dry white wine
4 medium-size Belgian endives,
    julienned
2 cups heavy cream
Salt
White pepper, freshly ground

Heat a heavy-bottom skillet and add clarified butter. Dredge veal in flour, place in skillet, and lightly saute on both sides. Remove veal to a warm plate and keep warm.

Discard butter from skillet, but do not wash. Add shallots and white wine. Cook until reduced to 2 or 3 tablespoons. Add endives, making sure not to brown or burn. Add heavy cream and cook slowly until sauce coats the back of a spoon. Season to taste and keep warm.

To serve, transfer veal onto four hot plates. Add any juices that remain from the veal to the sauce. Using a large tablespoon gently nap veal with sauce.

Sauteed string beans, cherry tomatoes, and Pomme Parisienne (small roasted potatoes) make for a great accompaniment.

MAKES 4 SERVINGS
Photograph, Page 23

THE PATIO RESTAURANT

3349 Piedmont Rd. NE, Atlanta, GA 30305; (404) 237-5878.

The Patio, a lovely French restaurant in Atlanta's Buckhead neighborhood, is small, intimate, and elegant right down to the hand-sewn lace on the linen napkins and the original art hanging on the walls. The Patio is a showcase for the owners' passion for perfection. Every vegetable, every sauce, every entree of seafood, meat, or fowl, must pass their exacting standards. The perfect place for quiet, unhurried conversation, and discriminating Atlantans have taken strongly to The Patio.

BLANQUETTE DE VEAU

3 1/2 pounds boneless best
　quality veal (pale) from leg
2 cups veal or chicken stock (see
　Basic Stocks)
1 bay leaf
1 teaspoon finely chopped fresh
　thyme, or 1/2 teaspoon dried
1 whole clove
1 cup white wine
4 tablespoons butter
1/4 cup flour
7 large egg yolks
1 1/3 cups whipping cream
2 tablespoons lemon juice
18 fresh pearl onions, poached
18 fresh mushroom caps,
　poached

Clean veal thoroughly of gristle. Cut into 1 1/2-inch squares.

In a saucepan combine veal, stock, bay leaf, thyme, clove, and wine and bring to simmer. Cook slowly, just a few bubbles breaking the surface, until tender, about 10 minutes (test a piece). If overcooked the meat will be dry. Remove meat and wash off scum. Strain liquid and place in a clean pot. Bring back to simmer.

In a separate saucepan melt butter and add flour, cook slowly to make a golden roux. Add to simmering liquid, stirring constantly until slightly thickened. Remove from heat.

In a bowl whisk egg yolks until fluffy. Add cream and lemon juice. Add this mixture to liquid slowly, stirring, and heat until it thickens enough to coat a spoon lightly. Add veal, poached mushrooms, and pearl onions.

May be reheated in a double boiler. Serve over buttered noodles.

MAKES 6 SERVINGS
Photograph, Page 20

THE PEASANT UPTOWN

Phipps Plaza, Peachtree and Lenox Rds. NE, Atlanta, GA 30326; (404) 261-6341.

When you have spent all morning or afternoon scouring treasure-laden shelves at Phipps Plaza for that perfect gift, or stunning new outfit for a special occasion, then it is time for a fine luncheon or dinner at The Peasant Uptown. Amid the wicker furnishings and the garden-like green and white decor, the friendly staff will beguile you with the day's selection of American and continental dishes for which Atlanta's Peasant Group has earned an enviable national reputation.

PASTRY LOG

6 ounces broccoli (cooked weight)
1 large puff pastry sheet
   (see Glossary)
6 ounces sliced ham
4 ounces Swiss cheese, sliced
$1/4$ cup egg wash (1 egg, beaten
   with 2 tablespoons water)
1 cup Hollandaise sauce
   (see Basic Sauces)

Steam broccoli for 1 to $1^1/_2$ minutes. Plunge into cold water, drain, and separate into stalks.
Place pastry on a baking sheet lined with parchment paper. Arrange ham slices down the center of pastry. Top with cheese slices, then arrange broccoli stalks over top. Enfold ingredients in pastry, sealing edges with egg wash. Turn seam-side down and brush with remaining egg wash. Refrigerate until serving time.
Before serving bake at 450 degrees F. for about 7 minutes. Reduce heat to 375 degrees F. and continue baking another 4 to 7 minutes until golden brown. Slice into 4 portions.
Serve each portion with a (2-ounce) ramekin of Hollandaise sauce.
MAKES 4 SERVINGS

SEA PALMS RESTAURANT

Sea Palms Golf & Tennis Resort, Frederica Rd., St. Simons Is., GA 31522; (912) 638-3351.

The Sea Palms Resort community nestles amongst the moss-draped live oaks of the 18th-century St. Clair Plantation on St. Simons, one of coastal Georgia's scenic "Golden Isles." Guests come to play championship-caliber golf, and tennis on all-weather courts. They also have a private stretch of Atlantic Ocean beach, a spacious clubhouse, and luxurious villa accommodations. Dinner in the Sea Palms Restaurant is highlighted by fresh seafoods, steaks, tempting desserts, and attentive service.

HOMARD AU VEAU, SAUTE

6 (5-ounce) lobster tails
6 thin slices veal medallions, about 1¼ pounds
Flour to dust
2 tablespoons butter
1 pound mushrooms, washed and sliced
½ cup dry Sauternes wine
2 tablespoons fresh, chopped parsley
2 tablespoons fresh, chopped garlic
Juice of 1 lemon
Salt and pepper

Remove lobster meat from shell and cut into 1½-inch pieces. Dust lobster and veal with flour.

In skillet heat butter and saute lobster lightly. Add mushrooms and continue cooking until mushrooms are tender.

Remove lobster and mushrooms with slotted spoon and set aside.

Saute veal in same skillet until golden brown on both sides, adding more butter if necessary.

Return lobster and mushrooms to skillet, add wine and flame (see Glossary).

When flames subside, add parsley, lemon juice, and garlic. Simmer for 2 to 3 minutes. Taste for seasoning, adding salt and pepper as necessary, and serve.

To serve place lobster and mushrooms over veal medallions.

MAKES 6 SERVINGS
Photograph, Page 18

THE SUNDIAL RESTAURANT

The Westin Peachtree Plaza Hotel, Peachtree St. at International Blvd. NE, Atlanta, GA 30343; (404) 659-1400.

All Atlanta spreads beneath your feet as you glide up to the Sundial in a glass-enclosed capsule that seems more like a spaceship than an elevator. Ensconced in the Sundial, you gently revolve about the 73rd floor of the Westin Peachtree Plaza, the world's tallest hotel. Stone Mountain and Kennesaw Mountain rise on the horizons. Matching the breathtaking scenery is the superb continental cuisine, which changes with the seasons like the scenery all about you.

MONGOLIAN BEEF

1 pound tenderloin beef tips
1/4 cup sesame oil
1/2 teaspoon crushed red peppers
1 garlic clove, minced
Salt and pepper to taste
1/2 cup sesame oil
3 tablespoons butter
1 1/2 tablespoons flour
Rosemary, thyme, majoram,
    chopped green onions to taste
1/4 cup Burgundy wine
1/2 cup beef stock (bouillon cube
    or see Basic Stocks)

Mix together 1/4 cup sesame oil, red peppers, garlic, and salt and pepper. Marinate the beef in this for 45 minutes.

After marinating, in a skillet, heat 1/2 cup sesame oil and saute meat until tender. Remove from heat and keep warm.

In a saucepan, melt the butter. Add the flour and stir in the herbs and green onions. Slowly add wine and beef stock. Bring to gentle boil and simmer for 5 minutes.

To serve place quarter of meat on each plate and cover with about 4 tablespoons of sauce.

MAKES 4 SERVINGS

Photograph, Page 22

SWISS TREATS RESTAURANT

Akers Mill Square, 2971 Cobb Parkway, Atlanta, GA 30339; (404) 952-1444.

Swiss Treats is a small, homey, European-style cafe located in the heart of one of metropolitan Atlanta's most thriving commercial/residential neighborhoods. Off busy U.S. 41, a short drive from Cumberland Mall and the Atlanta Galleria, the 50-seat restaurant features a variety of Swiss and French specialties for luncheon and dinner. Try one of the many cheese fondues, a delicious veal dish, salads, gourmet sandwiches and soups, topped by a creamy homemade pastry or torte. Wines and favorite cocktails complete a very continental repast.

STEAK DE VEAU "ST. MORITZ"
(Sauted veal steak with cepe mushroom sauce and spatzle)

1 ounce cepe mushrooms, dry
    (see Glossary)
2 tablespoons butter
1 medium-size onion, finely
    chopped
2 cloves garlic, minced
1 cup white wine
2 cups demi-glace (see Glossary)
1 cup whipping cream
Salt, pepper, paprika to taste
4 top round veal steaks, 1/2-inch
    thick, about 3 pounds
Flour to dust

Spatzle
1 1/2 cups flour
2 eggs
1 cup milk
Salt, pepper, nutmeg to taste
Water

Soak cepe mushrooms in lukewarm water to soften and then wash thoroughly.

Melt butter in a skillet and saute mushroom, onion, and garlic. Deglaze pan with wine and cook for a few minutes. Add demi-glace and cook for another few minutes. Remove from heat and add whipping cream. Season to taste with salt, pepper, and paprika.

Season veal steak with salt, pepper, and paprika and flour lightly. Saute in butter for about 5 minutes, turning once, cooking as desired. (Do not overcook.) Before serving, pour over cepe mushroom sauce.

To make Spatzle: Combine flour, egg, milk, salt, pepper, and nutmeg in a bowl, and mix to form a stiff dough.

In a large pot bring salted water to boil. Have another container with cold water ready beside it.

Make dumplings by putting small pieces of dough into hot water. When dumplings surface to the top, remove and put in cold water. When all dumplings are cooked, drain cold water. Before serving, saute spatzle in butter until golden brown, season with a dash of salt and pepper.

MAKES 4 SERVINGS

TRADER VIC'S

The Atlanta Hilton & Towers, Courtland & Harris Sts. NE, Atlanta, GA 30303; (404) 659-6200.

A touch of the South Seas in downtown Atlanta, Trader Vic's exotic menu is highlighted by roast suckling pig, and a tempting array of seafood, chicken, lamb, beef, and pork dishes dressed in pineapple, coconut, green pepper, peanuts, and other unusual garnishes. Guests relaxing in the Tahitian setting of bamboo, teak, and rattan furnishing, splashing waterfalls and green plants, can enjoy one of Trader Vic's Polynesian-style drinks. A great place for a special occasion escape from the everyday routine.

INDONESIAN LAMB ROAST

1/3 cup celery, finely chopped
1/3 cup onion, finely chopped
1 clove garlic, minced
3/4 cup oil
1/4 cup vinegar
2 teaspoons A-1 sauce
3 tablespoons curry powder
2 dashes Tabasco sauce
3 tablespoons honey
1 teaspoon oregano
2 bay leaves
1/2 cup prepared mustard
Juice and rind of 1 large lemon
6 lamb chops, or a rack of lamb
*   trimmed of fat*

Saute celery, onions, and garlic in oil until onion is transparent. Stir in remaining ingredients except lamb and simmer a few minutes. Chill. Marinate chops or rack of lamb in this mixture 3 or 4 hours in refrigerator, turning several times. Drain marinade from meat.

Wrap bones of chops or rack of lamb with foil, leaving meaty portions exposed. Arrange in greased, shallow baking pan. Brush meat with marinade and bake at 400 degrees F. for about 20 minutes, or longer, depending upon thickness of meat and desired tenderness. Turn meat once during baking period and baste frequently with marinade.

During the last few minutes of cooking, meat may be placed under broiler if further browning seems necessary.

Serve remaining marinade hot, as a sauce for meat.

MAKES 6 SERVINGS

"Man is what he eats."
LUDWIG FEUERBACH

POULTRY

ANNE MARIE'S
COUNTRY FRENCH CUISINE

3340 Peachtree Rd. NE, Atlanta, GA 30026; (404) 237-8686.

Atlantans and knowledgeable visitors from afar have made an institution of this suave corner of France in the heart of busy Buckhead. With its softly seductive lighting, fresh flowers, charming country-inn ambiance, and exquisite Gallic cooking, Anne Marie's is an ideal spot for conversation and conviviality, to woo a client or romance someone special. The French provincial menu of seafoods, veal, duckling, and steaks is prepared with a master chef's artistic hallmark.

CHEF STEVE MILES' CHICKEN A L'ORANGE

*1 orange, peeled, sliced, and
    seeded
1 cup frozen orange juice
    concentrate
3 cups demi-glace (see Glossary)
1/4 cup butter
4 (8-ounce) chicken breasts,
    boneless, skinned, sliced in
    1/2-inch strips
Flour to dust
1 cup onion, finely chopped
1 clove garlic, crushed
6 tablespoons Grand Marnier
1/2 cup whipping cream
Salt and pepper
Garnish: parsley and orange slices*

In a saucepan combine orange and orange concentrate and reduce, stirring occasionally. Add demi-glace and simmer for half an hour. Set aside.

Melt butter in skillet. Flour chicken and saute with onions and garlic. Add Grand Marnier and orange sauce to chicken and simmer for 20 minutes.

Before serving, add whipping cream and season to taste. Garnish with parsley and orange slices.

MAKES 4 SERVINGS

BEALL'S 1860

315 College St., Macon, GA; (912) 745-4768.

In 1865, owner Nathan Beall fled his lovely Greek Revival home just ahead of General William T. Sherman's Federal armies. Today, guests at Beall's 1860 enjoy the lovely ante-bellum surroundings of Nathan Beall's home while dining on excellent Southern specialties like chicken Francaise, fresh vegetables, steaks, and desserts at lunch and dinner. Beall's group dining and meeting facilities are among Macon's largest and finest.

CHICKEN FRANCAISE

1¹/₂ cups butter
¹/₄ cup lemon juice
¹/₂ cup dry vermouth
2 tablespoons soy sauce
Black pepper to taste
6 (8-ounce) chicken breasts,
    boned and skinned
¹/₃ cup green olives, chopped
¹/₃ cup celery, chopped
¹/₃ cup mushrooms, sliced
2 tablespoons cornstarch, plus
    enough water to make a paste
    the consistency of sour cream

In a large skillet, melt 1 cup butter over low heat. Stir in lemon juice, vermouth, soy sauce, and black pepper, and add chicken breasts. Cook over low heat for 30 to 40 minutes, or until chicken is tender. Remove chicken from pan and keep warm.

Add to the remaining ingredients in skillet remaining butter, olives, celery, and mushroooms. Simmer for 5 minutes. Thicken with cornstarch paste.

Serve chicken breasts over wild rice, topped with Francaise sauce.

MAKES 6 SERVINGS

BIG CANOE

Big Canoe, GA 30143; (404) 268-3333.

One of Georgia's most beautiful resort/residential communities, Big Canoe spreads across more than 5500 wooded mountain acres in Pickens and Dawson counties. Under its canopy of blue skies, Big Canoe offers a host of recreational pleasures from golf and tennis, to hiking or plain relaxing. Do your own cooking, or let the Big Canoe staff cater to you in the Sconti Clubhouse.

BONELESS STUFFED BREAST OF CHICKEN DIABLE

6 medium whole chicken breasts,
  skinned and boned
1 (10-ounce) package frozen
  chopped spinach
1/2 pound sweet Italian sausage,
  casings removed
1 green onion, thinly sliced
1/8 teaspoon freshly ground black
  pepper
Melted butter
Paprika

Diable Sauce
2 teaspoons finely chopped
  shallots
8 crushed peppercorns
3 ounces white wine or white
  vinegar
1 cup brown sauce (see Glossary)
1 teaspoon Worcestershire sauce
1/2 teaspoon chopped parsley

With meat mallet or dull edge of a French knife, pound each chicken breast until one-quarter inch thick.

Completely thaw spinach. Squeeze dry with paper towel.

In skillet cook sausage until well browned, breaking apart with fork. Drain well and toss with spinach, green onion, and pepper. Let cool. Place one chicken breast on work surface and sprinkle with a generous amount of spinach and sausage stuffing (about 1 1/2 tablespoons) to within a half-inch of the edges.

Fold the two long sides slightly towards the middle and roll chicken breast along its length, jelly-roll fashion. Fasten seam with two toothpicks.

Brush with melted butter and paprika and bake at 400 degrees F. for 40 minutes, or until chicken is fork tender, basting occasionally with pan drippings.

Pour Diable Sauce over and serve with boiled red potatoes or rice.

Diable Sauce
In a saucepan put shallots, peppercorns, and wine or vinegar and cook until reduced to a thick paste. Add brown sauce and Worcestershire sauce and strain through a sieve. Add parsley.

MAKES 6 SERVINGS

BLUDAU'S AT THE
1839 GOETCHIUS HOUSE

405 Broadway, Columbus, GA 31901; (404) 324-4863.

On a tree-shaded bluff above the Chattahoochee River, the Goetchius House had been one of Columbus' most elegant residences dating back to 1839. Today, this gracious home is a fine restaurant, specializing in American, French, and continental cuisines, served in charming Victorian dining rooms. The Country Captain, an outstanding chicken dish, was created by a Columbus cook as a special treat for President Franklin Delano Roosevelt.

COUNTRY CAPTAIN *(A Goetchius House favorite)*

1 pound chicken breasts, about 4
1/2 cup flour
Salt and pepper
1/4 cup butter
1/2 onion, diced
1/2 green pepper, diced
1/2 clove garlic, minced
1 teaspoon curry powder
2 to 3 tomatoes, peeled and diced
1/2 teaspoon parsley, chopped
Pinch powdered thyme
2 tablespoons raisins
1 1/2 cups cooked rice
Garnish: 1/2 cup toasted, diced
    almonds, parsley, and
    additional raisins

Remove skin from chicken breasts and bone if desired. Season with salt and pepper and dredge in flour.

In a skillet melt butter and saute chicken until brown. Remove chicken from pan and place in casserole.

In the same skillet using the same butter, saute onion, green pepper, and garlic. Season with salt, pepper, and curry powder (to taste). Add tomatoes, parsley, thyme, and raisins. Simmer for five minutes.

Cover the chicken in the casserole dish with the sauce. Bake in a moderate 350-degree-F. oven for 30 to 45 minutes.

Cook the rice according to the package directions.

Line a platter with rice. Place the chicken on top and sprinkle with diced almonds, parsley, and raisins.

MAKES 4 SERVINGS

COUNTRY PLACE
AT COLONY SQUARE

Peachtree and 14th Sts. NE, Atlanta, GA 30361; (404) 881-0144.

Politicians, performers, Memorial Arts Center patrons, office workers, and local and visiting celebrities keep the Colony Square "branch" of Atlanta's Peasant Group humming all the time. The spacious Mediterranean dining rooms and comfortable lounge are known for consistently delicious American/continental cuisine at lunch, dinner, and Sunday brunch. After performances at the Arts Center, Atlantans relive the experience over cocktails and late supper, while a pianist plays for their enjoyment.

GINGER DUCKLING

1 pound honey
$^1/_2$ cup soy sauce
2 cups sherry
$1^1/_2$ ounces fresh ginger, peeled and grated
2 cloves garlic, peeled and crushed
3 ducks, defrosted
$1^1/_2$ teaspoons Kosher salt
1 teaspoon white pepper
Duck drippings as available from roasting duck
$^1/_4$ cup cornstarch
2 cups water

To prepare marinade: Combine honey, soy sauce, sherry, ginger, and garlic in a saucepan. Heat over low flame to dissolve honey; set aside. Spread ducks with salt and pepper. Roast at 425 degrees F. for 20 minutes; prick skin with tines of a fork. Reduce oven heat to 325 degrees F. and continue roasting 3 hours. As ducks roast, baste 3 times with $1^1/_2$ cups of marinade.
Cool and split ducks in half, lengthwise. Refrigerate until ready to serve.
To prepare sauce: Bring remaining marinade to boil; strain off garlic. Combine cornstarch with water or with degreased duck drippings. Add to marinade and simmer until thickened.
To serve: Reheat duck halves at 350 degrees F. for 30 minutes or until heated through. Ladle 4 tablespoons sauce over each portion.
MAKES 6 SERVINGS
Photograph, Page 18

DAVIS BROTHERS CAFETERIA

Georgia State Farmers Market, Forest Park, GA 30050; (404) 366-7414.

Located within striking distance of the bountiful fruit and vegetable stalls of the State Farmers Market, Davis Brothers features delicious southern homecooking in a pleasant, friendly atmosphere. Along with an array of fresh vegetables, Davis Brothers' specialties include fried chicken, roast beef, fresh strawberry shortcake and cobblers, and savory chicken and dumplings, all served with garden-fresh vegetables and salads. These tasty dishes can also be enjoyed at Davis Brothers Cafeterias all over Georgia and Florida.

CHICKEN AND DUMPLINGS

2 (5- to 6-pound) hens, cut into
    pieces
2$1/2$ quarts water
Yellow food coloring, optional
4 cups flour
5 tablespoons margarine
1 egg
$1/2$ cup ice water
Salt and pepper to taste
More flour as needed
Garnish: hard-cooked eggs,
    chopped pimiento, parsley

In a large stockpot (8-quarts), place hens with water. Cover and simmer for about 2$1/2$ hours or until meat is tender. Remove hens from pot, saving stock. Skin, remove meat from bones, cut meat in about 2-inch pieces. Yellow food coloring may be added to stock, if desired.

Put flour in mixing bowl. Cut in margarine and add egg and ice water. Add salt and pepper to tase. Form into 1 or more balls.

On a well-floured board with a floured rolling pin, roll out dough for dumplings as thin as possible. With a sharp knife, cut dough diagonally into dumplings about 1$1/2$- to 2-inches in size. (Chill at least 1 hour before cooking.)

Bring remaining stock to simmer and drop dumplings, a few at a time, into stock. Maintain simmer and stir while cooking. Cook approximately 20 minutes.

To serve, place dumplings in bottom of serving dish and top with chicken, that has been reheated in stock. Thicken remaining stock (see Note). Correct seasoning to taste, and pour over chicken and dumplings. Garnish with shredded hard-cooked eggs, diced pimiento, and chopped parsley if desired.

Note: Dumplings will scorch if cooked over high heat. Just maintain simmer. For thicker stock make roux (see Glossary), add 1 cup chicken stock gradually, and return to remaining stock.
MAKES ABOUT 10 SERVINGS
Photograph, Page 24

THE FARMHOUSE RESTAURANT

Holiday Inn — Thomasville, U.S. 19 South, Thomasville, GA 31792; (912) 226-7111.

The turn of the century was Thomasville's "Golden Age," an opulent few decades when Northerners came to spend the winter at lavish resort hotels and plantations. Modern-day guests, who come to this charming south Georgia city to visit the beautiful homes and gardens and participate in the April Rose Festival, may enjoy the comforts of the Holiday Inn and the fine Southern cuisine at the Farmhouse Restaurant, which features quail, catfish, fried chicken, and a host of vegetables and breads.

PLANTATION BREAST OF CHICKEN SAUTE

4 chicken breasts, boned
6 tablespoons butter
12 fresh medium mushroom caps
³/₄ cup dry sherry
³/₄ cup light cream
4 (¹/₄-inch thick) slices of
    cooked ham
2 cups cream sauce (see below)
1 tablespoon pimiento
Salt and pepper
4 (3- by 3-inch) squares puff
    pastry (see Glossary)
Garnish: parsley

In a large ovenproof skillet in half butter saute chicken, skin side down, until golden brown. Turn chicken over and add mushrooms. Cook 5 minutes more. Pour off excess drippings. Add half sherry, half cream, ham slices, cream sauce, pimiento, and salt and pepper to taste. Cover and bake at 350 degrees F. for 30 minutes or until chicken is tender.

Quarter puff pastry diagonally and place in each of 4 individual skillets or au gratin dishes. Place a slice of ham over each and top with a chicken breast and a few mushrooms.

Add remaining butter, sherry, and cream to sauce in skillet. Blend well with wire whisk and cook 2 to 3 minutes over medium heat. Strain sauce and pour over chicken.

Cover each dish with foil and bake at 400 degrees F. for 10 minutes. Garnish with parsley.

Cream Sauce

Melt quarter cup butter over low heat. Blend in quarter cup all-purpose flour, half teaspoon salt, and dash white pepper. Add 1³/₄ cups light cream all at once. Cook and stir over medium-high heat until mixture thickens and bubbles. Makes 2 cups.

Note: Homemade cornbread can be substituted for the puff pastry to give a delightful change of taste.

MAKES 4 SERVINGS

GENE & GABE'S

1578 Piedmont Ave., NE, Atlanta, GA 30324; (404) 874-6145.

In the early sixties, Gene & Gabe's helped introduce Atlantans to the glories of Northern Italian cuisine. Creamy pastas, veal and seafoods draped in delicately herbed sauces, luscious desserts, and Italian wines found an immediate home among discriminating diners. Over the years, this intimate dining room, with its subdued lights, original art works, soft music from a grand piano, and gracious service has enhanced its mystique and solidified its most-favored status with Atlantans, visiting celebrities, and a former United States president.

CHICKEN GABRIEL

1/2 pound ground Italian sausage
2 cups cooked wild rice
1/4 teaspoon minced garlic
1 teaspoon minced parsley
1 cup bread crumbs
2 eggs
6 chicken legs, not thighs, deboned, keeping meat in 1 piece.
1/4 cup sherry
Juice of 1/2 lemon
1 cup chicken stock (see Basic Stocks)
Salt and pepper to taste
Garnish: fresh chopped parsley

Saute sausage until about half done, drain off grease and dry with paper towel. Combine with wild rice, garlic, parsley, bread crumbs, and eggs. Blend well. Stuff into deboned chicken legs and bake in a pan with about quarter of an inch of water in it for 45 minutes at 350 degrees F., turning at least once.

Remove from oven and put pan drippings into a saucepan. Add sherry, chicken stock, lemon, and salt and pepper to taste. Reduce by about one-quarter. Pour over stuffed legs and top with parsley for garnish.

MAKES 6 SERVINGS

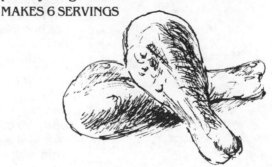

K.C.'S PAN FRIED CHICKEN

234 Hilderbrand Drive, Sandy Springs (Atlanta), GA 30328; (404) 256-2115.

Housed in a turn-of-the-century home, with rustic wooden beams, barn-sided walls and a cozy neighborhood bar, K.C.'s *tour de force* is perfectly seasoned chicken, pan-fried to a golden crisp in big iron skillets. Other specialties of this friendly house are fresh Georgia mountain trout, succulent steaks, fresh vegetables, and an array of home-baked breads, biscuits, muffins, and desserts. All this, within shouting distance of busy Roswell Road.

K.C.'S PAN FRIED CHICKEN

1 (2^1/$_2$- to 3-pound) chicken fryer,
  cut up
3 tablespoons salt
4 cups all-purpose flour
8 tablespoons ground pepper
Vegetable shortening (preferably
  Crisco)

Place chicken in a bowl and fill with cold water until covered, add 1 tablespoon salt, and soak for 1 hour.

Combine flour, remaining salt, and pepper in a bowl.

Preheat skillet filled half way with shortening to 350 to 375 degrees F.

Drain salt water from chicken and coat each piece completely with seasoned flour.

Place chicken in skillet and cook until golden brown, turning about every 10 minutes. Insure that the chicken is never covered with cooking oil.

For best results use a black cast-iron skillet and do not cover the chicken while cooking. Save the drippings to use in gravy.

Note: If you wish to make a gravy save pan drippings. Add to drippings in pan ^{1}/$_2$ cup flour and stir in thoroughly to tighten up. Gradually add 1^1/$_2$ cups hot water with a little chicken stock or bouillon cube. Simmer until it thickens. Thin with little milk or cream for creamy consistency. Season with salt and white pepper to taste.

MAKES 2 TO 3 SERVINGS

MICHELLE'S

Georgia-Pacific Center; 133 Peachtree St. NE, Atlanta, GA 30303; (404) 529-9400.

Step off Atlanta's busy Peachtree Street, into the Old World richness of marble, brass, exquisite glass sculpture, music, flowers, elegant table settings, and service as knowledgeable as you would find in Vienna or Paris. Michelle's, in a greenhouse overlooking Margaret Mitchell Square downtown, features the very finest continental cuisine, drawn from both the classic and *nouvelle* repertoire. Adjacent to the dining room, nightly jazz in the lounge provides the ideal setting for drinks and conversation.

BREAST OF DUCK WITH PEPPER AND FIGS

4 duck breasts
1/2 cup butter
1 tablespoon shallots, chopped
1 tablespoon brandy
1 cup demi-glace sauce
  (see Glossary)
Salt and pepper
1 tablespoon green, red, and black
  peppercorns
4 fresh figs
1 cup red wine
3/4 cup sugar
Rind of 1 orange, julienned
Rind of 1 lemon, julienned
4 red tomatoes, peeled, seeded,
  and diced
1 pound fresh spinach, sauted in 1
  teaspoon butter

Trim duck breasts. In a skillet, melt 1 tablespoon butter and sear breasts; brown on both sides. When breasts are cooked, place them on a serving platter and slice. Keep warm.
Add shallots to skillet and saute. Deglaze juices with brandy, add demi-glace. Slice remaining butter into 4 pieces and individually whisk into sauce. Correct seasoning and add peppercorns. Poach figs in red wine and sugar with orange and lemon rind for 10 minutes. Fill with fresh diced tomato. Reduce wine in pan and glaze figs.
To serve, coat duck with sauce. Garnish with figs filled with the tomatoes and fresh spinach sauted in butter.
MAKES 4 SERVINGS
Photograph, Page 22

PANO'S & PAUL'S

1232 West Paces Ferry Rd. NW, Atlanta, GA 30327; (404) 261-3662.

Owners Pano Karatassos or Paul Albrecht bid you a warm welcome to their sybaritic world of Edwardian appointments, brass and glass, and private dining booths curtained with Victorian fabrics. They and their polished staff invite you to enjoy the finest European and American wines as you dine on exquisite French, Swiss, German, and other continental cuisines. Veal sweetbreads, lobster Cardinal, and Viennese tortes swaying under waves of whipped cream are only a few of the delights awaiting guests at this special place.

LES SUPREMES DE POULARDE EN DAUBE

2 chicken breasts, halved,
    skinned, and boned
Salt and pepper
Flour to dust
1/2 cup clarified butter
    (see Glossary)
1/2 cup all-purpose flour
1 cup chicken stock (see
    Basic Stocks)
4 tablespoons heavy cream
3 ounces sweetbreads, precooked
2 ounces chanterelles
    (see Glossary)
2 tablespoons walnut halves
2 tablespoons Calvados (French
    apple brandy)
8 ounces puff pastry
    (see Glossary)
1 egg, lightly beaten

Sprinkle chicken breasts with salt and pepper. Dust very lightly with flour. In a saute pan melt clarified butter and saute chicken until brown. Remove chicken breasts and place in a casserole with a lid.

Blend the flour into remaining butter in skillet and saute for 2 to 3 minutes or until smooth. Add chicken stock, heavy cream, salt, and pepper to taste and strain into a fine china cup.

Place sweetbread morsels, chanterelles, and walnut halves into casserole with chicken breasts. Pour sauce over all and sprinkle on Calvados.

For a special presentation cover casserole with lid and seal the lid around edges with one-quarter-inch thick puff-pastry dough, cut 2 1/2-inches-wide.

Decorate sealing pastry with cut outs from dough scraps. Brush dough with beaten egg and bake in preheated oven at 375 degrees F. for 12 to 14 minutes.

Cut away sealing pastry to free casserole lid. Serve dish including some of the pastry.

MAKES 4 SERVINGS

THE PLANTERS

250 Garrison Rd., Marietta, GA 30060; (404) 427-4646.

In 1848, Marietta's first mayor, John Heyward Glover, built this magnificent Greek Revival mansion as a centerpiece for his Bushy Park Plantation. Today, Mayor Glover's splendidly restored home, set amidst 13 landscaped acres, is known as The Planters. Here, surrounded by antiques and classical architecture, diners enjoy five-course dinners drawn from every American regional cuisine. Before or after dinner, guests may relax in the Victorian splendor of the lounge.

TURKEY STEAK

6 (4-ounce) raw turkey breasts
   (sliced 1/4- to 1/2-inch thick)
1 cup sherry
1 teaspoon thyme
1 teaspoon salt
1 teaspoon white pepper
6 large eggs
1 1/2 cups whole milk
1 cup sliced chopped almonds
1 cup dry bread crumbs
1/2 cup Parmesan cheese, grated
4 tablespoons butter
4 tablespoons flour
1 quart chicken stock (see Basic
   Stocks)
1 cup heavy whipping cream
1 cup carrots, julienned
1 cup onions, sliced thin in rounds
   (separate in half)
1 cup celery, julienned
Butter

Brush turkey slices with mixture of 1 tablespoon sherry, thyme, salt, and pepper.

Beat eggs, add milk, place in a flat dish.

Combine almonds, bread crumbs, and Parmesan cheese on a sheet pan covered with wax paper.

Dip turkey slices into egg mixture and then into crumb mix. Place on a platter and chill. Save egg mixture.

For sauce, in a large saucepan, melt butter and add flour. Gradually add 2 cups chicken stock. Bring to boil and add remaining sherry, chicken stock, salt and pepper to taste. Simmer gently for about 10 minutes. Heat cream and add to sauce over low heat, until mixture is smooth and well combined.

Dip turkey slices in egg mixture again. Saute in butter until tender, about 10 to 15 minutes. Saute vegetables in butter, salt, and pepper to taste, until tender but firm.

To serve, place sauce on plates, then turkey steaks; pour remaining sauce on top, and garnish dish with julienned vegetables.

MAKES 6 SERVINGS

SAUTEE INN COUNTRY GOURMET RESTAURANT

Highways 17 and 255, Sautee, GA 30571; (404) 878-2940.

High on a hill, in the cool green mountains of northeast Georgia, the Sautee Inn surrounds its guests with an atmosphere of quiet leisure, reminiscent of earlier times. In this charming setting, diners serve themselves from a bountiful buffet that includes a selection of traditional southern favorites given the spice of variety by continental dishes prepared by hosts John and Emily Anthony. A charming place to highlight your visit to Alpine Helen and the other beautiful attractions in the mountains.

TROPICAL CHICKEN WINGS

4 pounds chicken wings
Flour
Salt and pepper
2 tablespoons water
2 tablespoons vegetable oil
Melted butter or margarine
1 (1-pound) can pineapple tidbits
$1/2$ cup brown sugar
$1/2$ cup white wine
1 cup pineapple juice
2 teaspoons cornstarch
1 cup onions, julienned
1 cup green peppers, julienned
Slivered almonds

Prepare chicken wings by trimming off tips and cutting wings into two parts. Dredge chicken with flour that has been seasoned with salt and pepper. Put water and oil into $9^1/2$- by 13-inch baking dish. Add chicken in one layer. Brush with melted butter or margarine. Bake uncovered at 400 degrees F. for about 25 to 30 minutes, until golden brown.

Drain juice from pineapple into small saucepan. Add sugar, wine, additional pineapple juice, and cornstarch. Cook until thickened and clear. Add onions, peppers, and pineapple tidbits. Spoon mixture over wings and sprinkle with almonds. Continue to bake until thoroughly hot, about another 15 minutes.

MAKES 6 SERVINGS

SEASONS THE STEAK CLUB

Lanier's Ramada Inn Central, 418 Armour Drive NE, Atlanta, GA 30324; (404) 873-5213.

At the Seasons, the finest prime steaks are cooked to perfection over charcoal embers. Diners also have a choice of a constantly changing selection of entrees, slow-roasted on a rotisserie. Fresh seafoods and international specialties are other highlights of the Seasons' menu. Diners' enjoyment is enhanced by an elegant candlelit atmosphere of warm colors, rich fabrics, and fresh flowers on every table. Delectable croissants, breads, and desserts are prepared daily.

BREAST OF CHICKEN VICTORIA

4 (7-ounce) boneless chicken
    breasts, skinned and split in 2
    pieces
Salt and pepper
8 (1¹/₂-ounce) pieces Alaskan king
    crab leg meat
¹/₂ cup butter
Flour for dusting
2 teaspoons shallots, finely
    chopped
2 cloves garlic, finely chopped
4 large mushrooms, sliced
8 canned artichoke hearts,
    quartered
4 teaspoons dry white wine
4 teaspoons lemon juice

Pound chicken pieces to approximately quarter-inch thick. Season with salt and pepper. Lay pieces flat on work table. Lay one piece of crab across width of each breast. Roll each breast lengthwise around crab meat and secure with toothpicks to hold roll. Dust rolled breasts lightly with flour.

Melt butter in an aluminum pan, add breasts, and saute until lightly browned on all sides. Save drippings.

Transfer chicken to a baking pan and bake in oven at 325 degrees F. for 10 minutes. Transfer to warm plate.

Reheat drippings in aluminum pan, adding 2 teaspoons butter if needed. Add shallots and garlic and saute for 3 minutes until lightly browned. Add mushrooms and saute for a further 3 minutes. Add artichokes and saute for 2 minutes. Then add wine and lemon juice. Mix all ingredients in pan, pour over chicken breasts, and serve hot.

MAKES 4 SERVINGS
Photograph, Page 18

A TASTE OF CHINA

Harris Tower, 233 Peachtree St. NE, Atlanta, GA 30303; (404) 659-6333.

A Taste of China, a well-known Hong Kong restaurant, has made its debut in downtown Atlanta's exciting Peachtree Center, and is a destination for those who relish the adventure of outstanding oriental cuisine. The sumptuously decorated restaurant offers a menu drawn from five provincial Chinese cooking styles. Peking duck, barbecued to a crisp golden turn, is available without advance notice. The adjoining Oriental Express Art Gallery is laden with treasures from every corner of Asia.

PEKING DUCK

1 (4¹/₂-pound) Peking Duck
5 tablespoons soy sauce
1 teaspoon red wine vinegar
1 cup water
5 cups flour
¹/₂ cup glutinous rice flour
   (see Note)
2¹/₂ teaspoons salt
1 teaspoon monosodium
   glutamate
1 teaspoon oil
Sesame oil
8 cups oil
¹/₂ cucumber, cut into sticks
8 green onions, whites only
Hoisin sauce (see Note)

Clean the duck, cutting a hole under a wing to remove the innards. Coat the skin with a mixture of the soy sauce, vinegar, and ¹/₂ cup water. Hang duck for 2¹/₂ hours or until dry. Roast in oven at 400 degrees F. for 20 minutes.

Make a dough combining the flour, rice flour, salt, and monosodium glutamate with a little water. Add 1 teaspoon oil and mix thoroughly. Roll out the dough very thin and cut into circles 5 inches across. Brush 1 side of each with a little sesame oil. Put them together in pairs, oil side inwards. Cook the pairs in an ungreased skillet for 1¹/₄ minutes on each side until they puff up and the surface bubbles. Carefully separate the pancakes.

In a wok, heat 8 cups of oil until boiling and, holding the duck above the wok, keep pouring the oil over it until it turns golden brown.

Serve the pancakes, cucumber sticks, green onions, and hoisin sauce on separate plates. Carve the duck in thin slices arranging the skin pieces and meat pieces separately.

To eat, spread a pancake with hoisin sauce, add duck slices, cucumber, and onion sticks, and roll tightly. Close 1 end by folding over the flap.

Note: Rice flour and hoisin sauce are available at oriental stores and some gourmet sections of grocery stores.

MAKES 2 SERVINGS
Photograph, Page 19

SEAFOOD

ANTHONY'S

3109 Piedmont Rd. NE, Atlanta, GA 30305; (404) 262-7379.

This gracious mansion was constructed by a wealthy Washington, Georgia, planter nearly two centuries ago. In the early 1970s, it was transplanted, brick by brick, plank by plank, to a wooded four-acre site off busy Piedmont Road. Handsomely decorated with antiques and art, Anthony's today relives the hospitality of yesteryear with superb American and continental cuisine, flawless service, wines, and your favorite libations. Come, relax, and spend a most enjoyable evening in the Old South of *Gone With the Wind.*

FILLET OF POMPANO *(Stuffed with crab meat, Sauce Bercy)*

4 pompano fillets (2 pompano)
1 pound fresh lump crab meat
2 shallots, finely chopped
Salt and pepper
Juice of 1 lemon (2 tablespoons)
1 tablespoon white wine
4 large sliced mushrooms
4 large lettuce leaves
1/2 cup butter
1 cup white wine
1/4 cup fish stock (see Basic
    Stocks)
2 green onions, chopped
1/2 cup whipping cream
3 tablespoons sherry
Cornstarch as needed
1 small zucchini, julienned
1 small carrot, julienned
1 small yellow squash, julienned
8 small red potatoes, cooked
    in skins
Garnish: parsley and lemon rings

Bone pompano. Make a pocket in each fillet. Mix crab meat with shallots, salt and pepper, lemon juice, and 1 tablespoon wine. Stuff in fillets' pockets. Top each with sliced mushrooms. Poach lettuce leaves in simmering salted water for a few seconds. Do not allow water to boil. Remove leaves and place in cold water to stop cooking. Drain and set aside.

Put 1/4 cup butter in bottom of baking dish. Place fish in dish, add additional white wine and fish stock. Cover each fillet with a lettuce leaf, top with remaining butter and bake in oven at 375 degrees F. for 10 minutes. Remove from oven, set aside, and keep warm.

Put juices from pan in heavy skillet, add onions, whipping cream, and sherry. Reduce sauce about one-third. If necessary thicken with sprinkling of corn starch.

Blanch julienned vegetables in salted boiling water. Vegetables must stay crisp.

To serve, top fish with julienne of vegetables and sauce. Garnish with potatoes, parsley, and lemon rings.

MAKES 4 SERVINGS

BENNIE'S RED BARN

5514 Frederick Rd., St. Simons Island, GA 31522; (912) 638-2844.

Coming to St. Simons and having dinner at The Red Barn is as important to many regulars as walking on the beaches of this Georgia Golden Isle. This comfortable hideaway, with its old timbers and candlelight, has been a coastal institution since 1954, when it was opened by Bennie Gentile. The Red Barn delights its guests with charbroiled steaks, broiled local seafoods, and delicious desserts. Even in warm weather, couches around the big fireplace are the most popular seats in the house.

CRAB AU GRATIN RED BARN

¹/₂ cup butter
1 cup plain flour
3 cups milk
¹/₂ teaspoon Tabasco sauce
¹/₂ teaspoon Worcestershire sauce
1 pound crab meat
¹/₄ pound mild Cheddar cheese, grated
Cheese and paprika to top

In a 2-quart saucepan melt butter. Gradually add flour and brown well. Slowly add milk, and stir until mixture is blended. Then add Tabasco and Worcestershire sauces, stirring vigorously. Check crab meat for pieces of shell, then add to the mixture, stirring steadily as added. Finally add cheese and stir until completely melted. Cook 5 minutes at medium heat.

Serve as is, or in a casserole dish. Sprinkle lightly with more cheese and paprika and broil until cheese melts and is lightly browned.

MAKES 4 SERVINGS

BLANCHE'S COURTYARD

440 King's Way, St. Simons Island, GA 31522; (912) 638-3030.

Where do St. Simons' residents repair for an enjoyable evening of dining? Many of them forget their troubles in the bayou-Victorian surroundings of Blanche's Courtyard, a whimsical hodge-podge of buildings centered around a 300-year-old oak tree. Each weekend a rollicking ragtime band beats out the good old tunes, while guests regale in seafood delights, fried chicken, and steaks, finished off with a praline sundae, a glorified brownie, or some other exotic topper.

BLUE CRAB STUFFING

¹/₃ cup margarine
¹/₂ cup onion, chopped
¹/₂ cup celery, chopped
¹/₃ cup green pepper, chopped
2 cloves garlic, minced
¹/₂ cup pimiento, chopped
1 pound crab meat
2 cups bread crumbs
3 eggs, beaten
1 teaspoon seafood season, or to taste (see Note)
1 teaspoon salt
¹/₂ teaspoon pepper
4 to 5 pounds flounder fillet
Butter

In a skillet melt margarine. Saute onion, celery, green pepper, and garlic until tender. Add pimiento, crab meat, bread crumbs, and eggs. Mix well and season to taste.

In individual, buttered casserole dishes place 3 to 4 ounces of flounder. Fill with 3 ounces of stuffing and top with another 3 to 4 ounces of flounder. Dot with butter.

Bake at 350 degrees F. for about 15 minutes or until flounder flakes easily with a fork.

Note: McCormick's is best, but is very hot, so be careful.

MAKES 8 to 10 SERVINGS

THE BOULEVARD RESTAURANT

Radisson Inn Atlanta, I-285 at Chamblee-Dunwoody Rd., Atlanta, GA 30338; (404) 394-5000.

Situated on I-285 in the heart of one of the metropolitan area's most desirable business and residential sections, the Radisson Inn is one of the city's most popular suburban hotels. Guests stay in 391 tastefully decorated rooms, with easy access to tennis, swimming, a health club, and some of the area's largest and most modern meeting facilities. Dining rooms include the Boulevard Restaurant, which specializes in excellent American and continental dishes, cocktails and wines.

SHRIMP PIERRE RADISSON

*12 potato balls scooped from new
    potatoes
2 tablespoons clarified butter
    (see Glossary)
1 teaspoon shallot, finely chopped
1 teaspoon garlic, finely chopped
3 artichoke bottoms, quartered
12 shrimp (16 to 20 count),
    peeled and deveined
1/4 cup white wine
Dash lemon juice
Garnish: parsley*

Cut out potatoes with a melon ball scoop. Blanch in boiling water.

Heat clarified butter in a saucepan. Add potatoes and cook until brown. Add shallots, garlic, artichoke bottoms, and shrimp. Continue cooking until shrimp are pink, about 3 to 7 minutes depending on size. Add wine and lemon juice.

Garnish with chopped parsley. Serve over rice.

MAKES 2 SERVINGS
Photograph, Page 22

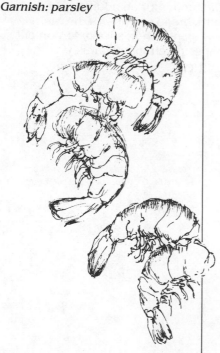

THE BUGATTI RESTAURANT

Omni International Hotel, One Omni International, Atlanta, GA 30335; (404) 659-0000.

Off the main lobby of the Omni International Hotel, Bugatti is a sumptuous dining experience. Ensconced on plush green banquettes, surrounded by dark wood paneling and gleaming brass, guests enjoy excellent Northern Italian cuisine, from creamy pastas, to osso bucco, marvelous veal dishes and frothy desserts like zuppa inglese. Bugatti's Sunday Brunch is a feast you'll long remember, with virtually the entire Northern Italian cookbook laid out in irresistible splendor.

GAMBERONI ALLA DIAVOLO *(Broiled Large Shrimp with Diavolo Butter)*

30 large shrimp
1 cup butter, softened
1 clove garlic, chopped
Juice of one lemon
1 teaspoon crushed red pepper
1 tablespoon brandy
1 teaspoon fresh parsley, chopped
Salt and pepper to taste
3 cups fresh bread crumbs
Garnish: lemon slice and chopped
    parsley

Peel and butterfly shrimp. Devein and wash shrimp. Place in a casserole and season with salt and pepper.

To make Diavolo Butter, in a bowl combine butter, garlic, lemon juice, red pepper, brandy, parsley, and season with salt and pepper.

Top the shrimp in the casserole dish with Diavolo Butter. Place casserole under the broiler for 5 to 7 minutes.

Remove and sprinkle with bread crumbs. Place back under the broiler for an additional 1 to 2 minutes, or until bread crumbs are brown.

Serve with garnish of lemon slice or lemon cut into a star-shape and chopped parsley.

MAKES 6 SERVINGS

CAFE DE LA PAIX

Atlanta Hilton & Towers, Courtland & Harris Sts. NE, Atlanta, GA 30303; (404) 659-2000.

A charming country French decor, greenery, rattan and art prints turn this corner of the busy Atlanta Hilton into a quiet retreat for breakfast, luncheon and dinner. Following a sumptuous breakfast buffet, midday fare features colorful salads and a constantly changing selection of hot entrees. In the evening, you're invited to sample from an à la carte selection of entrees, wines and desserts, with live entertainment to accentuate your dining pleasure. An elegant place after business, after shopping, or after theater.

SUPREME DE SAUMON MODERNE, SAUCE VERTE
(Poached Salmon Steak, Sauce Verte)

4 (8-ounce) boneless salmon fillets
1 quart fish bouillon (see Note
    and Glossary)
2¹/₄ cups dry white wine
10 drops lemon juice
1¹/₂ teaspoons seasoned salt
¹/₄ teaspoon white pepper
¹/₂ cup parsley juice (see Note)
1 pint heavy cream
1 teaspoon cornstarch

Poach salmon fillets in bouillon for 10 minutes or until the fish flakes with a fork. Remove fish, place in warm oven (about 200 degrees F.) on serving platter. Reserve bouillon.

To the bouillon add white wine, lemon juice, salt, white pepper, and parsley juice (for coloring). Simmer mixture on low heat until liquid has been reduced by one-half.

Add cream and simmer for 8 minutes, then thicken with cornstarch. This will not affect the taste.

Remove salmon from warming oven, pour sauce over salmon, garnish with chopped parsley and serve.

Note: Chicken bouillon may be substituted for fish bouillon, but it should be diluted by 50 per cent.
To make parsley juice, place fresh parsley in blender with about 2 tablespoons water. Blend until green liquid results.

MAKES 4 SERVINGS

COTILLION ROOM

Holiday Inn Downtown, 175 Piedmont Ave. NE, Atlanta, GA 30303; (404) 659-2727.

Near the center of downtown Atlanta, a short walk from great restaurants, entertainment, shopping, and the dynamic Peachtree Center office complex, the Holiday Inn Downtown is on I-75 and I-85, and convenient to all parts of booming metropolitan Atlanta. Guests enjoy beautifully appointed guest rooms, superb meeting facilities, a swimming pool, and other luxuries. For dining and entertainment, the Cotillion Room offers excellent breakfasts, luncheons and dinners, with your favorite cocktails and wines.

SHRIMP TARRAGON WITH SEA SHELL ROYAL

4 tablespoons butter or margarine
1¹/₂ pounds shrimp, peeled and
   deveined
4 tablespoons flour
¹/₂ cup clam juice
3 teaspoons lemon juice
¹/₄ cup Sauternes
1 (10-ounce) can condensed
   cream or milk
Dash salt and white pepper
¹/₂ teaspoon powdered onion
1 teaspoon tarragon
Chopped parsley

Sea Shell Royal
¹/₂ cup green onions, sliced
   (no tops)
3 tablespoons margarine
12 ounces hot cooked shells,
   macaroni
¹/₂ cup mushrooms
Dash salt and pepper
Garnish: chopped parsley

Melt butter in saucepan and saute shrimp about 5 minutes. Stir in flour and gradually add clam juice, lemon juice, and Sauternes. Cover and cook about 5 more minutes. Add condensed cream or milk, salt and pepper, powdered onion, and tarragon. Simmer until thickened. Sprinkle with parsley and serve with Sea Shell Royal.

To make Sea Shell Royal: Saute onions in margarine until golden. Add macaroni shells, mushrooms, salt, pepper and parsley. Serve hot.

MAKES 6 SERVINGS

W. D. CROWLEY'S
RIVERHOUSE & TAVERN

8849 Roswell Rd. NE, Atlanta, GA 30338; (404) 993-5039.

In the early 1970s, an ambitious group of young Atlantans came up with an idea for a new kind of restaurant. It would have a dapper environment, offer great mixed drinks, and a cross-section of foods from hearty hamburgers, to soups, salads, lobster tails, steaks, and prime rib. There would be an atmosphere of hospitality and good fun. The idea was a sensation, and now Crowley's Riverhouse is a main port of call for North Fulton County's discriminating winers and diners, meeters and minglers.

HERB-STUFFED TROUT

6 boneless rainbow trout
2 bay leaves
1 small shallot, sliced
2 sprigs parsley, chopped
1/2 cup wine vinegar
1/2 cup water
4 peppercorns
1 1/2 cups bread crumbs
1 egg, beaten
1 tablespoon chives, chopped
Salt and white pepper to taste
1/4 cup melted butter
1 tablespoon capers
Juice of 1 lemon

Place trout in a shallow glass container. Mix bay leaves, shallot, parsley, wine vinegar, water, and peppercorns and pour over trout. Marinate trout in refrigerator overnight. Drain trout and reserve liquid.

Combine bread crumbs, egg, chives, and salt and white pepper to taste. Stuff the cavity of each trout and brush each with melted butter. Bake in 375-degree-F. pre-heated oven for 20 minutes.

Heat reserved marinade and add capers and lemon juice. Ladle this mixture over trout at serving time.

MAKES 6 SERVINGS

DAILEY'S

17 International Boulevard NE, Atlanta, GA 30303; (404) 681-3303.

Dailey's, a part of the Peasant group, is in a brick-walled converted department store warehouse in the heart of downtown Atlanta's hotel and shopping district. Diners may sit either on the first floor, which has live nightly entertainment, or in the handsomely decorated main dining room upstairs. Either way, it is a delightful experience, and downtown shoppers often drop by for one of their scrumptious desserts displayed like the crown jewels.

SEA TROUT PHYLLO

1/4 cup clarified butter
   (see Glossary)
4 (8-ounce) boneless sea
   trout fillets
6 ounces shredded carrots
6 ounces grated onions
2 teaspoons garlic, finely minced
Salt and pepper to taste
12 sheets phyllo pastry
   (see Glossary)
Melted butter
1/2 cup egg wash (1 egg and 2
   tablespoons water, beaten)
Hollandaise sauce (see
   Basic Sauces)

Put clarified butter in large skillet and heat until very hot. Sear fish 30 seconds (or longer depending on thickness) on each side until fish is barely opaque. Remove fish from skillet; reduce heat to low.

Cook carrots and onions in same skillet. Season fish with garlic, salt, and pepper, and cover with vegetables.

Preheat oven to 375 degrees F.

Brush 3 sheets of phyllo with melted butter and stack them. Continue making buttered stacks of 3 phyllo leaves for each fillet.

Wrap each fillet in phyllo lengthwise, enclosing it completely. Shape the phyllo so that it resembles a whole fish. (Round the top and pinch it two inches from the bottom for the tail.) Brush each with egg wash.

Bake for 15 to 20 minutes until golden.

Serve with Hollandaise sauce.

MAKES 4 SERVINGS

THE DELEGAL ROOM

King and Prince Beach Hotel, 201 Arnold Rd., St. Simons Is., GA 31522; (912) 638-3631.

The King and Prince Beach Hotel has symbolized the relaxed hospitality of St. Simons Island for more than four decades. The mellow Spanish Colonial hotel sits at the edge of its own Atlantic Ocean beach, with the murmur of the waves as a ceaseless panacea. The Delegal Dining Room, adorned with stained-glass murals, offers a sumptuous selection of fresh seafood, steaks, and continental dishes, all served with delicious views of the sea. The adjoining tavern is the perfect place for drinks and conversation.

SEAFOOD STRUDEL

2 tablespoons unsalted butter
2 tablespoons all-purpose flour
1/2 teaspoon Dijon-type mustard
Salt
Tabasco sauce
1 cup milk, room temperature
1 cup fresh bread crumbs
1/4 teaspoon Parmesan cheese, freshly grated
1/4 teaspoon dry mustard
1/2 pound puff pastry (see Glossary)
1 pound cleaned, shelled, cooked crab, shrimp, (see Glossary), lobster, or halibut; or combination, in bite-size pieces
1/2 cup Swiss cheese, grated
2 hard-boiled eggs, chopped
3/4 cup sour cream
1/4 cup parsley, chopped
1/4 cup onion, diced
2 tablespoons chives, chopped
1 large garlic clove, minced
1 egg, beaten with 1 tablespoon water (egg wash)
Minced parsley
2 tablespoons Parmesan cheese, freshly grated
Garnish: crab or lobster claws, optional

Melt 2 tablespoons butter in small saucepan over low heat. Stir in flour to make smooth paste and heat gently, stirring constantly, until mixture just begins to bubble. Remove from heat, add mustard, pinch of salt and Tabasco. Slowly stir in milk. Place over medium heat and cook, stirring constantly, until mixture bubbles and thickens. Taste for seasonings and adjust if necessary. Cover and chill until very thick and firm, about 2 hours.

Preheat oven to 375 degrees F., lightly butter baking sheet. Combine bread crumbs, Parmesan, and dry mustard in small bowl. Roll out puff pastry thinly and cut into 6 (6-inch by 6-inch) squares. Layer on seafood and sprinkle with Swiss cheese and chopped egg. Dot with sour cream. Sprinkle with parsley, onions, chives, garlic, and bread crumb mixture and dot with chilled sauce.

Gather edges of pastry, moisten with egg wash and press down to seal. Turn strudel over and place on prepared baking sheet. Brush tops of strudels with remaining egg wash.

Bake at 375 degrees F. for 15 to 20 minutes or until pastry is golden brown. Transfer to warmed serving platter, dust with more Parmesan and minced parsley. Garnish with crab or lobster claw or whole shrimp if desired.

MAKES 6 SERVINGS
Photograph, Page 20

THE DIPLOMAT

230 Spring St. NW, Atlanta, GA 30303; (404) 525-6375.

The Diplomat is a sumptuous haven for American and continental cuisine, cocktails and wines. The plush decor, knowledgeable service, and assured air of professionalism conspire to create a memorable luncheon or dinner. An orchestra playing for dancing and entertainment adds to your enjoyment. It's located in the heart of downtown Atlanta's hotel and convention district, a few steps from the Merchandise and Apparel Marts.

SOLE DIPLOMAT

4 (12-ounce) fillets of sole
10 tablespoons clarified butter
   (see Glossary)
3 cups fresh white bread crumbs
1/2 cup water

Sauce Diplomat
2 tablespoons shallots, chopped
1 cup vermouth
1/2 cup white wine
1 tablespoon beef glaze
   (see Glossary)
2 cups butter, softened
Salt and pepper to taste
2 teaspoons lobster, diced

Place fillets of sole in a baking pan with clarified butter and bread crumbs on top and brown under broiler.

Add water and bake at 350 degrees F. for 10 minutes. Remove fillets and keep warm. Save pan liquid for sauce.

To make Sauce Diplomat: Add shallots to liquid left in baking pan, along with vermouth, white wine, and beef glaze. Reduce until almost dry. Beat butter and add it with salt and pepper to reduced sauce. Strain. Add lobster and saute it briefly in butter.

To serve, put Sauce Diplomat on a platter and set sole on top.

MAKES 8 SERVINGS

DON JUAN'S SPANISH CASTILLIAN RESTAURANT

1927 Piedmont Circle, Atlanta, GA 30324; (404) 874-4285.

Come into this attractively decorated stucco cottage and enjoy a vicarious journey to Old Spain. From the Basque Country comes such as pata de cordero (lamb), from the sunny Mediterranean coast, there's zarzuela a la Catalana, seafoods in a tangy broth. Or try their paella, with rice and an array of seafoods. These and other unusual dishes are redolent with the aromas of garlic and fragrant spices and complemented by a large selection of Spanish wines and sherries.

PAELLA DON JUAN

1/2 cup olive oil
3 cloves garlic
1/2 medium onion chopped
1 tomato, peeled and chopped
1 green pepper, chopped
Salt and pepper to taste
Pinch saffron to taste
Pinch of oregano and rosemary
1/4 pound pork, cut in pieces
1 (1/2-pound) chicken, cut in pieces
1/4 pound squid, chopped
1/4 pound veal, cut in pieces
1 pound rice
1 cup fish stock (see Basic Stocks)
1 cup chicken consomme
4 cups water
1 pound fresh mussels
1/2 pound fresh medium shrimp
1 pound small fresh clams
2 lobster tails, cut in half
1 pound crab meat, chopped
1 cup green peas for garnish
Red pimiento slices for garnish
1/4 pound chorrizo (Spanish sausage, see Note)
Garnish: lemon or lime wedges

Heat oil in large heavy-bottomed pan or paella pan. Add garlic, onion, tomato, and green pepper, and saute until brown. Season with salt, pepper, saffron, oregano, and rosemary.

Add pork, chicken, and squid, and cook for 5 minutes on medium heat. Add veal and cook for a further 2 minutes.

Add the rice and stir for 2 minutes. Then add fish stock, chicken consomme, and water. Cook 10 minutes. Add mussels, shrimp, clams, lobster, and crab. Cook for a further 10 minutes until rice is tender.

Decorate with peas, pimiento, chorrizo sausage slices on top of dish. Add lemon wedges on the edge of the pan as additional garnish.

Note: Available from gourmet meat stores or Spanish groceries or substitute Italian sausage.

MAKES 4 SERVINGS

EMMELINE AND HESSIE'S

St. Simons Causeway, St. Simons Island, GA 31522; (912) 638-9084.

Around the turn of the century, vacationers came to the moss-draped Golden Isle of St. Simons on ferryboats called *The Emmeline* and *The Hessie*. Today, the hospitable feeling of these two beloved boats is carried on by the Emmeline and Hessie Seafood Restaurant. Overlooking the picturesque Golden Isles Marina, the restaurant serves a tempting array of oysters, shrimp, crabs, and fish from local waters in an atmosphere of natural wood, greenery, and light.

HOT PEPPERED SHRIMP

2 cups margarine, softened
1/2 cup grated onion
1 tablespoon paprika
1 tablespoon black pepper
1 tablespoon bitters
1 tablespoon garlic powder
2 tablespoons seasoned salt
1 tablespoon dry mustard
1 tablespoon Worcestershire sauce
2 tablespoons wine vinegar
Shrimp, peeled and deveined, as
    needed

In mixing bowl or food processor beat margarine until light. Add remaining ingredients, except shrimp, and beat until well blended. Store covered in refrigerator until needed.

For Peppered Shrimp, heat 2 tablespoons of the "butter" in a small frying pan. When it starts to bubble, stir in 6 to 8 medium shrimp, per person. Stir quickly for 2 to 3 minutes until shrimp are just cooked.

Pour into a warm soup plate with the juices from the pan and serve with pieces of French bread for dipping into sauce.

MAKES UP TO 24 SERVINGS

GANTT'S

P.O. Box 605, St. Simons Island, GA 31522; (912) 638-4300.

Gantt's is a place of conversation and relaxation in the world of tranquility of St. Simon's Island. The sun, the ocean, the majestic live oaks, and the aura of its history dating back to Georgia's early days seem to generate a healing magic. Shrimp, oysters, and other delicacies from surrounding waters, another important part of the Island's "cure," are served at Gantt's in delicious abundance, along with prime steaks and homemade pies and cakes, accompanied by friendliness and attentive service.

FISHERMAN'S SKILLET

4 to 8 corn cobettes, "squared-off" ears of corn, about 3 inches
Milk, butter, salt
4 littleneck clams
2 Florida lobsters
12 ounces lump or claw crabmeat
Paprika
1 cup melted butter
8 tablespoons onion, finely chopped
8 teaspoons melted butter
White wine as desired
24 peeled shrimp, with tails on
24 medium-size scallops
8 oyster shells, well cleaned
Garlic salt
24 oysters
Tartar sauce, drawn butter, lemon, and baked potato for accompaniment

Boil cobettes in 1 part milk, $^1/_3$ part butter, enough to cover, with salt to taste for about 5 minutes.

If clams are frozen, bake for 2 minutes so they will open easily. Wash sand out of clams and return to 350-degrees-F. oven and bake until done, about 5 minutes.

Clean lobsters and remove meat from shell, starting at the big end. Pull tail from shells, but leave tip of meat attached. Put meat back into shells. Be sure lobsters are cleaned well, then fill large end with crabmeat stuffing. Sprinkle paprika onto white meat, then ladle 1 cup melted butter onto tails, getting some between meat and shell. Bake at 350 degrees F. for about 15 minutes until done.

Place onion in a skillet, add additional melted butter; brown onions. Add white wine as desired, bring to a simmer and add shrimp and scallops. Stir and turn as needed.

Place oyster shells in oven to get hot.

Sprinkle shrimp and scallops lightly with garlic salt, and when almost cooked, add oysters. Do not overcook oysters, they will be ready in seconds. Remove from skillet and set aside. Drain off excess cooking juices, but leave bottom of skillet coated. Place lobsters on skillet, place oysters inside shells, add shrimp, scallops, clams, and corn.

Serve with tartar sauce, drawn butter, lemon, and baked potato.

MAKES 4 SERVINGS

H.P.'S

Sheraton Savannah Inn & Country Club, 612 Wilmington Is. Rd., Savannah GA 31410; (912) 897-1612.

For more than half a century, the Savannah Inn and Country Club has been the *grande dame* of the Georgia coast, a quiet retreat on Wilmington Island, where harried city-dwellers could come to play golf and tennis, swim and relax in the sun, and enjoy coastal seafoods at their very finest. All this, and the resort is only a fifteen-minute drive from downtown Savannah's magnificent squares, ante-bellum mansions, and unique shops.

LOBSTER SAVANNAH

1 (1¹/₂- to 2-pound) lobster
¹/₂ teaspoon salt
Dash white pepper
1 tablespoon butter
¹/₄ cup diced green pepper
¹/₂ cup sliced, fresh mushrooms
1 whole pimiento, diced
1 teaspoon paprika
2 tablespoons sherry
1 cup white sauce (see
    Basic Sauces)
2 egg yolks
¹/₄ cup fresh bread crumbs
¹/₄ cup Parmesan cheese

In enough boiling water to cover, place lobster and simmer for 20 minutes. Remove, drain, and cool.

Split lobster down back and body so that it can be opened up. Crack claws so that meat is accessible.

Remove meat from tail and cut into cubes, season with salt and pepper, and saute in butter. Add green pepper, mushrooms, pimiento, paprika, and sherry. Saute for a few more minutes.

Beat egg yolks and fold into cooled white sauce. Heat until mixture thickens and remove from heat.

Combine with lobster mixture. Place back into lobster shell and sprinkle bread crumbs and Parmesan cheese on top. Bake at 375 degrees F. for 15 minutes or until the top is golden brown.

MAKES 1 SERVING

JIM WHITE'S HALF SHELL

2349 Peachtree Rd. NE, Atlanta, GA 30305; (404) 237-9923.

Friendly and informal, with a snappy nautical air, Jim White's Half Shell has been a major port o' call for Atlanta seafood fanciers for nearly 15 years. Oysters, jumbo shrimp, crab, red snapper, and other delicacies are flown in fresh daily from the Florida Gulf Coast. Trout comes from streams in the nearby north Georgia mountains and is prepared in several delicious ways, including New Orleans-style Pontchartrain. The bar is always lively.

TROUT PONTCHARTRAIN

1 cup of butter
Flour
4 (7-ounce) fresh trout fillets
2 ounces fresh lump crabmeat
2 cups diced, peeled tomatoes
4 tablespoons diced green onion
Dash salt and pepper
Dash oregano
Dash lemon juice
Dash garlic powder
Garnish: parsley and $1/2$ lemon

Melt butter in saute pan. Dust trout in flour and saute quickly in hot butter until done. Remove from pan and keep warm.
Saute other ingredients quickly and place over trout.
Garnish with chopped parsley and a half lemon.
MAKES 4 SERVINGS
Photograph, Page 22

JOE DALE'S CAJUN HOUSE

3209 Maple Dr., NE, Atlanta, GA 30305; (404) 261-2741.

Come into these cozy premises and savor owner Joe Dale's Louisiana Cajun specialties. Making a choice is often difficult. Tonight, will it be chicken and shrimp jambalaya, or will it be oysters or shrimp, that come in all manner of dress? Before enjoying your entree, you'll be treated to enormous servings of salads with Joe's marvelous house dressing, red beans, "dirty" rice, garlic bread, and potatoes. The piano bar adjoining is filled with regulars and rollicking music.

BARBECUED SHRIMP, NEW ORLEANS STYLE

1 pound raw shrimp, with shell
  (preferably with heads on —
  see Note)
1 tablespoon black pepper,
  cracked
1 tablespoon black pepper, finely
  ground
1 teaspoon leaf oregano
2 teaspoons monosodium
  glutamate
1 tablespoon seasoned salt
1 tablespoon parsley, finely
  chopped
2 teaspoons onion salt
4 to 6 tablespoons butter
1 tablespoon olive oil

Pat shrimp dry. Mix peppers, oregano, monosodium glutamate, salt, parsley, and onion salt and thoroughly toss shrimp in mixture. Let stand 1 hour. (At this time, if you prefer a very piquant sauce, add a little more finely ground black pepper.)

Place shrimp in casserole, add butter and olive oil. Bake at 400 degrees F. for 10 to 15 minutes, turning several times to coat with butter and oil. When cooked, peel and eat, using fresh French bread to soak up the gravy.

Note: Shrimp should be large, at least under 15 to the pound. We prefer shrimp with head on as the tomalley contained in the head portion imparts a very fine flavor. However, headless shrimp, which are easier to find, may be substituted. This recipe may also be used as an appetizer or hors d'oeuvre.

MAKES 2 SERVINGS
Photograph, Page 18

JOHNNY HARRIS RESTAURANT

1651 Victory Dr., Savannah, GA 31404; (912) 354-7810.

Generations of Savannahians have danced and romanced under the domed sky-blue ceiling, a-twinkle with electronic stars, in Johnny Harris' marvelous round main dining room. The Big Band Era still lives here on weekend nights, when the floor is packed with dancers young and old. Natives and visitors also flock to this friendly landmark, patterned after an old English country tavern, for first-class barbecue, seafood, and fried chicken so delicious it should be patented.

SHRIMP DE JONGHE

1 clove garlic, finely chopped
2 tablespoons shallots, finely chopped
2 tablespoons onions, finely chopped
$1/3$ teaspoon dried tarragon
$1/3$ teaspoon dried parsley
$1/2$ cup creamed sweet butter
1 cup bread crumbs
$1/2$ cup sherry
Salt, pepper, thyme, nutmeg to taste
$1 1/2$ pounds shrimp, peeled, deveined, and cooked
Buttered crumbs to top

In a large bowl, combine garlic, shallots, onion, tarragon, parsley, butter, bread crumbs, and sherry. Season to taste with salt, pepper, thyme, and nutmeg.
In six individual casseroles arrange alternate layers of shrimp with butter compound. Top with buttered crumbs.
Bake at 450 degrees F. for 15 to 20 minutes.
MAKES 6 SERVINGS

McKINNON'S LOUISIANE

2100 Cheshire Bridge Rd. NE, Atlanta, GA 30324; (404) 325-4141.

Ask native Atlantans for a list of their favorite dining places, and McKinnon's Louisiane will invariably be prominently featured. Since 1972, this nationally-awarded corner of Old New Orleans has also enjoyed a national reputation for the finesse of its Creole cuisine. Start your vicarious journey through the Vieux Carre with a piquant dish of seafood gumbo, and wend your way magically through great dishes that feature fresh oysters, shrimp, flounder, crab, and trout.

TROUT MEUNIERE

1 cup lightly salted butter
1 teaspoon freshly ground pepper
4 tablespoons fresh lemon juice
    (or 2 tablespoons lemon juice
    plus 1 tablespoon tarragon
    vinegar)
1/2 bunch parsley, chopped
4 (6- to 8-ounce) fillets of
    speckled trout (or salt water
    weakfish, or snapper, redfish,
    scamp, etc.), skinned
Flour, seasoned with salt, black
    pepper, pinch cayenne pepper
Vegetable oil
Garnish: parsley and
    lemon wedges

To make Meuniere sauce, melt butter over low heat until slightly browned. Add pepper, lemon juice, and parsley and set aside.

Add enough oil to cover skillet 1/8 inch deep. Coat fillets in seasoned flour. Over moderate heat, saute trout, two at a time. Lay fillets in pan, rib side first. When nicely browned, turn over and cook several minutes more.

Serve immediately topped with Meuniere sauce. Garnish with parsley and lemon wedges.

Note: The secret of this dish is the extremely simple Meuniere (pronounced moon-year) sauce, which can comfortably dress any other broiled, baked, or pan-fried fish.

MAKES 4 SERVINGS

THE MANSION

179 Ponce de Leon Ave. NE, Atlanta, GA 30308; (404) 876-0727.

"The Ornaments Of A Home Are The Friends Who Frequent It." In the spirit of this inscription over their stone hearth, the Richard C. Peters family welcomed guests to their Queen Anne-style mansion on Ponce de Leon Avenue in the 1880s. The same spirit of warmth and genuine hospitality greets diners today at one of Atlanta's most charming restaurants. In a series of fascinating rooms, guests can imagine themselves in the Victorian era, while enjoying fine American and continental cuisine and wines.

STUFFED FLOUNDER "ORLEANS"

4 ounces lump crabmeat
4 ounces bay shrimp
4 ounces scallops
2 cups dry white wine
Dash sherry
4 tablespoons sliced mushrooms
4 teaspoons green onions, green
    part only, thinly sliced
1 1/4 cups butter
4 cups heavy cream
4 teaspoons melted butter
4 teaspoons flour
Salt and pepper
Dash nutmeg
4 pounds fresh whole flounder
    (have butcher clean, removing
    fins, head, and dark skin)
4 tablespoons Hollandaise sauce
    (see Basic Sauces)

Poach crabmeat, shrimp, and scallops in wine and for extra taste add a dash of sherry, until done, about 2 minutes. Remove seafood and keep warm.

Reduce poaching liquid to one-fourth. Reserve. In skillet saute mushrooms and onions in 1/4 cup butter.

In saucepan bring cream to simmer. Combine 4 teaspoons melted butter and flour to form roux. Add roux to cream to thicken and let simmer 4 to 5 minutes. When smooth, add poaching liquid and season to taste with salt, pepper, and nutmeg. Simmer 2 minutes more. Add seafood, mushrooms, and onions.

Melt 1 cup butter in skillet and saute flounder 4 to 5 minutes on each side. Remove fish from skillet and bone. Fill the flounder with creamy stuffing and reshape. Top with Hollandaise and place fish under broiler until sauce is lightly brown.

Serve with light seasonal vegetables and boiled potatoes.

MAKES 4 SERVINGS

MICHELLE'S

Georgia-Pacific Center, 133 Peachtree St. NE, Atlanta, GA 30303; (404) 529-9400.

Michelle's is a glamorous star in Atlanta's dining crown, and an exquisite culinary experience savored with equal enthusiasm by residents and out-of-towners alike. Gorgeously situated in a greenhouse setting overlooking downtown Peachtree Street and Margaret Mitchell Square, Michelle's French/continental menu features many classical dishes, and many others created by the European staff. Before or after dinner, enjoy cocktails and live music in the Art Deco-style lounge. Luncheon at Michelle's is also the talk of the town.

FISH TERRINE WITH FENNEL SAUCE

2 pounds salmon
3 egg whites
1 pint heavy cream
Salt and pepper
2 pounds sea bass
4 egg whites
1 pint heavy cream
1 pound fresh spinach
8 fillets of sole, about 13 ounces
*   each*
¹/₄ cup port wine
¹/₂ cup white wine
1 cup mayonnaise
10 ounces fresh fennel julienned
2 tablespoons Pernod
*   (see Glossary)*
Garnish: 2 tomatoes, peeled,
*   seeded, and chopped*

Salmon Forcemeat: Blend salmon in blender. Add egg whites one at a time, then add cream and seasoning.

Sea Bass Forcemeat: Blend sea bass in blender. Add egg whites one at a time, then add cream and seasoning.

Parboil spinach in plenty of boiling salted water; cool it and press out all the water. Blend in blender with 4 ounces of sea bass forcemeat. Coat fillets of sole on their flattened side with a thin layer of spinach and sea bass forcemeat. Roll them up. Stand them upright in a buttered saucepan to poach with port and white wines. Poach them in a moderate 350-degree-F. oven, for about 10 minutes.
Put the salmon forcemeat in a pâté mold. In the center add the roulades of sole, cover with sea bass forcemeat. Cook in a moderate 350-degree-F. oven for about 1 hour. Serve cool on a bed of fennel sauce.

To make Fennel Sauce: Add Pernod and fennel to mayonnaise.
To serve put tomato around terrine.
MAKES 15 SERVINGS
Photograph, Page 18

MULBERRY INN

601 East Bay St., Savannah, GA 31401; (912) 238-1200.

The Mulberry Inn brings back to life the warmth and charm that characterized Savannah's hospitality in the ante-bellum days when cotton barons entertained in opulent mansions. Located near the historic riverfront, many of the Inn's 104 guest rooms and 29 suites are furnished with authentic antiques, some dating all the way back to the 18th century. Employees dress in period costume, and the dining room, with its chandeliers and lovely tableware, features exquisite Low Country cuisine.

SEAFOOD OMELET

1 tablespoon milk
1 tablespoon butter
3 eggs
1 1/2 ounces shrimp
1 1/2 ounces scallop
Dash salt
Dash pepper
Dash garlic powder
6 tablespoons seafood sauce (see
  Basic Sauces)
1 shrimp, peeled and deveined
1 scallop

Place butter in small pan or omelet pan over medium heat. Mix eggs and milk in small bowl. Saute seafood in butter and add salt, pepper, and garlic. After 1 minute add egg mixture. Add 4 tablespoons seafood sauce. When omelet becomes firm fold in half.

Add 1 shrimp and 1 scallop to pan and saute. After 3 minutes place omelet on round plate. Add shrimp and scallop on top of omelet and top with remaining seafood sauce.

MAKES 1 SERVING

THE PAVILION

DeSoto Hilton Hotel, 15 West Liberty St., Savannah, GA 31401; (912) 232-9000.

Just as the DeSoto Hilton stands out in the heart of an historic city filled with many treasures, so does The Pavilion, a restaurant that blends Savannah's charms with a master chef's artistry in the preparation of regional and continental dishes. The Pavilion is a comfortable and inviting room, with the graciousness of wicker and ferns, service immediate and impeccable, and warm southern smiles abounding. Local seafoods are prepared to perfection, and The Pavilion's sumptuous Sunday Brunch is a Savannah hallmark.

SCALLOP QUICHE

1½ pounds bay scallops or sea
   scallops cut into quarters
2 tablespoons vermouth
2 tablespoons minced parsley
¼ teaspoon dried thyme
Salt and pepper to taste
1 (9-inch) unbaked pie shell
5 eggs, lightly beaten
1 cup light cream
Paprika

Sprinkle scallops with vermouth, parsley, thyme, and salt and pepper to taste. Fill pie crust with scallops mixture.

Mix eggs and cream and pour over scallops. Sprinkle with paprika.

Bake at 450 degrees F. for 10 minutes; reduce heat to 350 degrees F. and bake for 25 minutes more, or until knife inserted in center comes out clean.

MAKES 8 SERVINGS

THE PAVILION DINING ROOM

Stouffer's Pinelsle Resort Hotel, Lake Lanier Islands, Buford, GA 30518; (404) 945-8921.

Only an hour's drive north of Atlanta, Lake Lanier is a vast inland sea, around whose 700-mile shoreline weary city-dwellers recharge their batteries in a variety of relaxing ways. One of the most beautiful ways is at Stouffer's Pinelsle Resort Hotel, a luxurious retreat with golf, tennis, swimming, and boating. Overlooking the lake's green waters, the Pavilion Dining Room features outstanding American and continental cuisine, cocktails, wines, entertainment, and dancing.

CASSEROLE MEDITERRANE

1/2 pound sole, filleted and cut in strips
1 lobster tail meat, sliced
10 mussels
5 clams
6 ounces scallops
10 shrimp, peeled and deveined
Salt and pepper
Juice of 1/2 lemon
1 tablespoon Worcestershire sauce
Flour to dust
6 tablespoons butter
1 onion, finely chopped
6 tablespoons tomato puree
1/4 cup white wine
1 cup fish stock (see Basic Stocks)
1 tablespoon butter
1 tablespoon flour
1/4 cup heavy cream
Pinch tarragon

Season all seafood with salt, pepper, lemon juice, and Worcestershire sauce and dust with flour. In a skillet heat 6 tablespoons of butter, and saute seafood until tender. Remove from skillet and keep warm.

Add onions to skillet and saute. Then add tomato puree, white wine to glaze, then fish stock. Make a roux with flour and butter (see Glossary). Add roux to liquid mixture to thicken. Add cream and season to taste. Add tarragon. Arrange seafood on a platter and pour the sauce over. Serve with rice.

MAKES 4 to 5 SERVINGS
Photograph, Page 24

THE PEKING

Northeast Plaza, 3361 Buford Highway NE, Atlanta, GA 30329; (404) 634-2373.

Like an elusive treasure, The Peking is hidden away in a quiet corner of a northeast Atlanta shopping center. Ah, but the rewards for the many who happen upon this marvelous place are bountiful. From China's Hunan and Szechuan provinces comes an array of fascinating soups and entrees spicy with pepper, garlic, onions and other piquant flavors. More subtle, but equally intriguing Mandarin dishes, are artfully prepared as for the Emperor himself. No wonder Peking is such a big Atlanta favorite.

PEKING SHRIMP

Vegetable oil
20 large fresh shrimp, peeled and
  deveined
1/4 cup peas and carrots, diced
  (fresh or frozen)
10 snow peas, sliced in half-inch
  pieces
10 Chinese mushrooms, whole
10 water chestnuts, sliced
  (canned)
2 cloves garlic, minced
1 green onion, chopped
Salt and pepper to taste
2 tablespoons soy sauce
1 tablespoon sugar
1/2 cup tomato sauce
2 tablespoons white wine
1/6 cup chicken stock (see Basic
  Stocks)
1 tablespoon cornstarch
1 tablespoon water

In a wok or large skillet, heat vegetable oil and quickly cook shrimp for 1 to 2 minutes. Add peas, carrots, snow peas, mushrooms, and water chestnuts and stir fry for about 2 minutes. Remove shrimp and vegetables from wok and discard remaining oil.

Heat another 2 tablespoons oil and quickly stir fry garlic and green onion for about 2 minutes. Return shrimp and vegetables to pan with garlic and green onion. Add salt and pepper to taste. Add soy sauce, sugar, tomato sauce, wine, and chicken broth. Make a paste with cornstarch and water. Add as needed to shrimp for thickening.

MAKES 2 SERVINGS

PIRATES' HOUSE

20 East Broad St., Savannah, GA 31401; (912) 233-5757.

The Pirates' House has lots of tales to tell. The main building dates back to the mid-1700s when it was a seamen's tavern; Robert Louis Stevenson set part of *Treasure Island* in this labyrinth of rooms. Today's buccaneers find a treasure of fresh seafoods from Georgia's coastal waters, winding up their feast with a choice of thirty-six spectacular desserts and perhaps an after-dinner libation in the Rain Forest Bar, where storms break out on schedule, but no one ever gets wet.

SEAFOOD AU GRATIN

Casserole Sauce
2 cups milk
1 to 1 1/2 cups Cheddar cheese,
    grated
1/2 cup Cheez Whiz
1/2 teaspoon salt
Dash black pepper
1/4 cup all-purpose flour

1 pound crabmeat
1 pound cooked shrimp

To make Casserole Sauce, in a heavy saucepan mix 1 1/2 cups milk with 1/2 cup cheese, Cheez Whiz, salt, and pepper. Cook, stirring constantly, over medium heat until cheese melts and mixture boils.

In a separate bowl mix flour with 1/2 cup milk until smooth. Add to cheese mixture and stir until thickened. Simmer for 20 minutes. (If not using right away, place a piece of plastic wrap directly on surface of sauce to prevent a skin from forming.)

Preheat oven to 350 degrees F.

Combine crabmeat, shrimp, and Casserole Sauce and pour into 2-quart casserole.

Top with 1/2 to 1 cup grated cheese and bake until bubbly and cheese is melted, about 30 minutes.

This may be baked in individual casseroles also.

MAKES 4 to 6 SERVINGS

THE PLEASANT PEASANT

555 Peachtree St. NE, Atlanta, GA 30308; (404) 874-3223.

Cuisine, service and ambiance blend pleasingly together in this intimate candlelit room with its tiled floors, bare brick, and brassware. This flagship of Atlanta's own Peasant Group features an American/continental menu, presented by the waiter on a chalkboard, listing an ever-changing choice of innovative dishes. Since opening in 1973, The Pleasant Peasant has been one of Atlanta's most consistently popular dining places and is a must for out-of-towners in-the-know.

SCALLOPS PARISIENNE

¹/₂ teaspoon garlic powder
³/₄ cup dry white wine
8 ounces fresh sea scallops
³/₄ cup white sauce (see Basic Sauces)
¹/₂ cup Parmesan or Romano cheese, grated
2 tablespoons melted butter

Bring garlic powder and wine to a simmer in a skillet.
Add scallops and simmer gently for 3 to 5 minutes until barely cooked. Remove scallops and place in a shallow ovenproof casserole. Cover with white sauce.
Sprinkle with cheese and drizzle with butter.
Bake at 400 degrees F. for 15 to 20 minutes until golden brown on top.
MAKES 1 SERVING

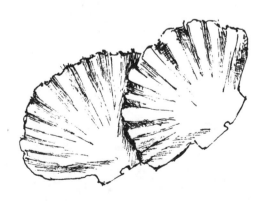

QUARTERS COURT

Guest Quarters, 111 Perimeter Center West, Atlanta, GA 30346; (404) 396-6800.

Guest Quarters Hotel at Perimeter Center provides 24-hour suite service, as well as intimate dining in its full service Quarters Court Restaurant. Breakfast and lunch offer both an a la carte menu and hot and cold buffets, with dinner being strictly a la carte. Luncheon buffets include a daily carved item such as the Salmon recipe provided below. A well balanced wine stock is maintained and all desserts, pastry, Danish, and rolls are baked daily at the hotel.

STUFFED SALMON WITH CHAMPAGNE SAUCE

1 tablespoon butter
2 pounds chopped spinach
1 medium onion or ¹/₂ cup
   shallots, chopped
4 cups cooked rice
4 cups cooked bay shrimp, peeled
   and deveined
Salt and pepper to taste
Seafood base to taste (see
   Glossary)
1 (8- to 10-pound) salmon, dressed
   and boned
¹/₂ cup butter
1 cup flour
2 quarts milk, scalded
¹/₂ bottle champagne
Garnish: parsley and
   lemon wedges

Melt butter in large skillet and saute spinach and onions or shallots together for 10 to 12 minutes. Add rice and shrimp, and season to taste.

Place stuffing in salmon, wrap salmon in foil, and bake at 350 degrees F. for 20 to 25 minutes. To make Champagne Sauce melt butter, add flour, and cook 5 to 10 minutes. Add milk and bring to a boil; simmer ¹/₂ hour. Season with salt and pepper, and add champagne.

To serve remove foil from fish, or simply open up foil, pour Champagne Sauce over fish, and garnish with parsley and lemon wedges.

MAKES 10 SERVINGS

THE RIVER HOUSE

125 River St. West, Savannah, GA 31401; (912) 234-1900.

A cotton warehouse built in 1810 is the setting for one of Savannah's most delightful dining experiences. With panoramic views of the Savannah River's heavy ship traffic to whet their appetites, River House guests enjoy oysters, shrimp, red snapper, flounder, and crabs from coastal waters, and lobsters, scallops, and other seafood delicacies flown in fresh daily. Luncheon and dinner patrons may also enjoy frosty Mint Juleps and Savannah's own libation, Chatham Artillery Punch.

SHRIMP CREOLE

1/4 cup margarine
4 ounces celery, sliced
3 ounces green pepper, sliced
4 ounces onions, sliced
1 clove garlic, pressed
18 ounces tomato paste
4 1/4 cups water
3/4 tablespoon sugar
3/4 teaspoon salt
1/2 teaspoon pepper
3/4 teaspoon monosodium
    glutamate
3/4 teaspoon thyme
6 whole cloves
1 1/4 bay leaves
1/2 cup flour
1/2 cup water
3 pounds shrimp, cooked, peeled,
    and deveined (see Glossary)

Melt margarine in skillet and saute vegetables and garlic until tender.

Add tomato paste and water. Then add sugar and seasoning. Put cloves and bay leaves in cheese cloth and place in sauce. Bring to boil and simmer for 30 minutes. Remove cloves and bay leaf.

Mix together flour and water to make a paste. Add to sauce. Simmer a further 15 minutes. Remove from heat.

Add shrimp to the Creole sauce. Serve with rice.

MAKES 6 to 8 SERVINGS

RUSTY SCUPPER

3285 Peachtree Rd. NE, Atlanta, GA 30305; (404) 266-0944.

At the Rusty Scupper, seafoods, steaks, prime rib, and other favorites are presented in a warm environment of natural woods, plants, glass, and an outdoor-like ambiance of pleasant informality. The restaurant's many contemporary levels are delightful places for drinks, dining, and conversation. Teriyaki shrimp, broiled Boston scrod, swordfish, and lobster tails are among the many seafood specialties. All dinners are accompanied by a house salad and warm honey-wheat bread with apple butter.

SOLE MONTEREY

8 (3- to 4-ounce) fillets Boston sole
$^1/_2$ cup butter
$1^1/_2$ teaspoons garlic powder
$1^1/_2$ teaspoons dried basil
1 teaspoon onion powder
$^1/_2$ teaspoon salt
4 ounces bay shrimp peeled
   and deveined
4 ounces crabmeat
1 cup Monterey Jack cheese,
   shredded
1 large tomato, peeled and diced
4 teaspoons Parmesan cheese

Pound fish fillets gently with a mallet.

In a skillet, melt butter. Add garlic powder, basil, onion powder, and salt. Remove from heat. Dip both sides of the sole into the warm seasoned butter mixture.

Place 4 pieces of sole on a greased sheet pan, skin side down. Next layer 1 ounce of shrimp and 1 ounce of crab meat on top of each piece of fish. Then top each with 1 ounce of shredded cheese. Top each with 1 ounce of diced tomatoes.

Slit the center of each remaining piece of fish with approximately a 2-inch cut. Place each of these four pieces of fish, skin side down, on top of the tomatoes and open up the slit to show the diced tomatoes on the layer below.

Sprinkle one teaspoon of Parmesan cheese over each serving.

Bake at 350 degrees F. for 20 to 25 minutes.

MAKES 4 SERVINGS

Photograph, Page 20

ST. ANDREW'S RESTAURANT

Augusta Hilton Hotel, 640 Broad St., Augusta, GA 30902; (404) 722-5541.

Downtown Augusta's largest and most luxurious hotel, the 216-room Hilton is a popular stopping place for business travelers, visitors to the city's many historical homes and sites, and fans who flock here every spring for the annual Masters Golf Tournament. Guests at the Augusta Hilton enjoy a complete health club, with racquetball and squash courts. Dining rooms and lounges serve varied menus of American and international dishes, cocktails and wines, with live entertainment and dancing.

GEORGIA SHRIMP GUMBO

$1/2$ cup butter
1 large onion, chopped
1 cup green pepper, chopped
1 pound fresh okra, sliced
1 pound small shrimp, cooked,
    peeled, and deveined
    (see Glossary)
3 fresh medium tomatoes,
    chopped
1 small (8-ounce) can whole corn,
    drained
1 small (8-ounce) can lima beans,
    drained
$1/8$ teaspoon black pepper
$1/8$ teaspoon salt
$1/2$ teaspoon monosodium
    glutamate
1 teaspoon chili powder

Prepare all ingredients.
In a saucepan, melt butter. Blend in all ingredients, bring to a boil, and simmer for 20 to 30 minutes, or until vegetables are just tender. Do not overcook. Overcooking will cause vegetables to blend together. Correct seasonings.
Serve on steamed rice or buttered noodles.
MAKES 4 SERVINGS
Photograph, Page 21

SAVANNAH FISH COMPANY

The Westin Peachtree Plaza Hotel, Peachtree St. at International Blvd. NE, Atlanta, GA 30343; (404) 659-1400.

One of Atlanta's most outstanding seafood restaurants takes its name from Georgia's historic port city. Through Savannah come blue crabs, shrimp, succulent oysters, and many varieties of fish that find their way to the tables. This beautiful dining room in the dramatic Peachtree Plaza hotel setting also draws its daily fare from the waters of Maine, the Gulf Coast, and Chesapeake Bay. Entrees are served with this tangy Savannah fish stew, and followed by Savannah hot puffs, pastry morsels adorned with cinnamon, whipped cream, and chocolate or vanilla sauce.

SAVANNAH FISH STEW

1/4 cup olive oil
1 leek, julienned
1 yellow squash, julienned
1 fennel root, julienned
1 onion, finely chopped
2 garlic cloves, finely chopped
1/4 teaspoon thyme
1/4 teaspoon marjoram
1/4 teaspoon saffron
Cracked black pepper
1 bay leaf
1 clove
1 cup white wine
Pernod to taste (see Glossary)
2 quarts fish stock (see
    Basic Stocks)
1 chicken bouillon cube
Salt to taste
Whole oysters, as many as desired
2 cups seafood, cubed (cod,
    flounder, shrimp, snapper,
    salmon)
1 large tomato, peeled, seeded,
    and diced
Garnish: fresh green fennel,
    chopped

In a large saucepan, heat olive oil. Add vegetables, garlic, herbs, and spices and saute all together, until tender.

Mix wine, Pernod, fish stock, and add bouillon cube and salt. Add to vegetables and bring to boil.

Place fish and tomato in heatproof serving dish. Pour boiling liquid with vegetables over the raw fish, and let sit for five minutes.

Sprinkle with chopped fennel and serve.

MAKES 4 SERVINGS
Photograph, Page 17

THE SHRIMP FACTORY

313 East River St., Savannah, GA 31401; (912) 236-4229.

While enjoying such delicious native seafoods as shrimp, crab, and oysters prepared in a variety of intriguing ways, guests at The Shrimp Factory can watch the ships of the world pass through Savannah's busy harbor. Specialties at this casual, friendly establishment are headed by such as shrimp Creole, crab and shrimp au gratin, stuffed flounder, and pine bark stew, a southern-style bouillabaisse prepared with five regional seafoods. Savory crab burgers are a big hit at lunchtime.

PINE BARK STEW *(Southern Bouillabaise)*

6 ounces celery
6 ounces onion
6 ounces green pepper
2 medium potatoes
3 quarts rich chicken stock (see
    Basic Stocks)
1 1/2 teaspoons thyme
3/4 teaspoon white pepper
3/4 teaspoon salt
1/2 cup margarine or butter
3/4 cup flour
12 ounces raw fish of choice
1/2 pound raw shrimp, peeled and
    deveined
1/2 pound raw crabmeat
1/2 pound raw scallops
1/2 pound raw oysters
3/4 cup dry sherry

Dice vegetables into 1-inch squares. Place with chicken stock and seasonings in pan, bring to the boil, and simmer until vegetables are tender, about 20 minutes.

In a separate pan melt margarine or butter, add flour, and simmer 5 minutes. Stir in soup, gradually. Add seafood and simmer for 10 minutes. Correct seasoning, to taste.

Remove from heat, add sherry, and serve.

MAKES 12 SERVINGS

THE STEEPLECHASE

Marriott Hotel Perimeter Center, 246 Perimeter Center Parkway, Atlanta, GA 30328; (404) 394-6500.

At the Steeplechase, guests are invited to come and enjoy a delightful dining experience aglow with the atmosphere of a southern hunt club. Authentic equestrian artifacts, photos, and prints enhance the warmth and comfort of the dining room. True to its surroundings, The Steeplechase offers a tempting selection of American steaks and seafoods, interesting continental dishes, wines and cocktails. The perfect place to relax after a hard business or shopping day.

SHRIMP ALMEDIA

1 green pepper, seeded and sliced
1/4 cup butter
1/4 cup sherry
1 1/2 ounces pimiento, diced
Salt and pepper to taste
1 1/2 cups milk
2 tablespoons flour
2 tablespooons butter
Dash thyme
1 pound shrimp, peeled, deveined, and cut in half lengthwise

Saute green pepper lightly in butter. Add sherry and simmer for 3 minutes. Add pimiento, salt, and pepper.

Bring milk almost to a boil. Melt butter in sauce pan, add flour and stir to make a roux. Add milk and continue stirring until sauce thickens. Add sauted green pepper and pimientos to sauce. Add shrimp and simmer for 3 minutes.

Remove from heat and serve over rice or pasta.

MAKES 6 SERVINGS

TASSEY'S PIER

3122 River Rd., Thunderbolt, GA 31404; (912) 354-2973.

A short drive from downtown Savannah's lovely historic district, Tassey's Pier invites you to sit by their big windows and watch the boats move in and out of the picturesque Thunderbolt Marina while you savor their excellent cuisine. Begin with oysters on the half shell, or crabmeat from Georgia and Carolina coastal waters. Then, in the glow of candlelight, enjoy fresh flounder, red snapper, or steaks prepared in owner Tassey Salas' special ways.

SHRIMP DOMOOZ

14 to 16 shrimp, about ²/₃ pound
1 egg, lightly beaten
1 pound lean medium hot pork
*   sausage (see Note)*
1 cup flour
1 cup evaporated milk
1 cup bread crumbs

Peel shrimp to last joint, leaving tail on. Butterfly (see Glossary) and devein.

Coat inside of shrimp with egg. Stuff each equally with sausage. Dust each with flour, then dip into evaporated milk, then into bread crumbs.

Fry in deep fat at 350 degrees F. until done or golden brown, about 3 to 5 minutes.

Note: Sausage must be very lean. If not, it will break out of the breading during frying.

MAKES 2 SERVINGS

THE TOWN TAVERN

15 Seventh St., Augusta, GA 30901; (404) 724-2461.

Since 1937, The Town Tavern has been downtown Augusta's foremost hall-mark of hospitality. In three ground-floor dining rooms, with an old English ambiance of cheery fireplaces, comfortable booths, and hunting prints, guests select from a menu that includes a delicious choice of appetizers, soups, seafoods, steaks, chops, and fowl. A pleasant place for all the family, The Town Tavern features a special children's menu, and is equally delightful at breakfast, lunch, and dinner.

FRESH SHRIMP CREOLE

1 stalk celery
2 large onions
4 bell peppers
1 cup margarine
4 (16-ounce) cans tomatoes
1 (16-ounce) can tomato juice
1 (28-ounce) can mushroom
   stems and pieces, drained
1/3 cup white wine
1 tablespoon salt
1 tablespoon cornstarch and
   enough water to make a paste
3 1/2 pounds cooked shrimp,
   peeled and deveined
   (see Glossary)
2 cups rice

Cut celery, onions, and pepper into pieces about the size of a half-dollar. Melt margarine in large pan, and saute vegetables until almost tender. Add tomatoes, tomato juice, mushrooms, wine, and salt, and simmer for 20 to 30 minutes. Make a paste with corn starch and water. Add slowly to tomato sauce until it thickens.

Cook rice according to package directions. Add shrimp to sauce and allow to heat thoroughly. Correct seasoning.

Serve over hot rice.

MAKES 12 to 14 SERVINGS

WINFIELD'S

100 Galleria Parkway, Atlanta, GA 30339; (404) 955-5300.

Winfield's is part of the Peasant Group, one of Atlanta's most acclaimed restaurant operations. Diners at Winfield's are surrounded by a pleasing contemporary decor of teal-green walls, spacious windows, plants, and original art works. The distinctive but always different Peasant Group cuisine features American and continental seafoods, steaks, Cornish hen, imaginative soups, and salads. Live entertainment is a centerpiece of the large, lively lounge, and you will find an unusual and unique menu of hors d'oeuvre.

BAKED PRAWNS

1 cup butter
1/2 pound onion, minced
1 cup green onions, finely chopped (1 bunch)
1/4 cup tomato paste
1/2 pound snow crab
1/4 teaspoon white pepper
1 teaspoon salt
1 cup bread crumbs
8 prawns, peeled, deveined, and butteflied (see Glossary)
1/2 sheet puff pastry (see Glossary)
Egg wash (1 egg, 2 tablespoons water)
Garnish: parsley sprig and lemon crown

Melt butter in skillet, add onions and green onions, cook 1 minute. Add tomato paste, crab meat, pepper, salt, and bread crumbs. Stir to combine and heat through. Cool.

Arrange butterflied prawns on a sheet pan in one layer. Portion 2 tablespoons stuffing mixture onto each prawn.

Cut pastry into 1-inch-long strips, about 1/2 to 1 inch wide. Brush sides with egg wash. Wrap each prawn in pastry with the seam on the top. Overlap edges and press to seal. Egg wash pastry.

Prebake prawns at 450 degrees F. for 10 minutes, reduce heat to 350 degrees F. for 5 minutes.

To serve, heat 2 prawns per serving for 5 minutes at 375 degrees F. until heated thoroughly. Place on large dinner plate with a parsley sprig and a lemon crown.

MAKES 4 SERVINGS

WINFIELD'S

100 Galleria Parkway, Atlanta, GA 30339; (404) 955-5300.

Winfield's is a crowning touch to one of Atlanta's most exciting commercial and entertainment complexes. The Atlanta Galleria is a stunning assortment of shops, restaurants, nightlife, office buildings and hotels. Winfield's complements the Galleria with imaginative continental and American cuisine, service, and ambiance that have made the Peasant group of restaurants synonymous with good living Atlanta style. The decor is highlighted by original art by Don Cooper, one of the city's finest young artists.

GRILLED SALMON STEAK

1/3 cup oil
1/4 teaspoon white pepper
2 cloves garlic, crushed
1 teaspoon garlic salt
6 (10-ounce) salmon steaks, 2
    inches thick
1 tablespoon juniper berries,
    coarsely ground (see Note)
1 1/2 teaspoons parsley flakes
1 parsley sprig per serving
1 lemon wheel per serving

Juniper Butter
3/4 pound butter
1 tablespoon parsley flakes
2 teaspoons juniper berries,
    coarsely ground

Combine oil, pepper, garlic, and garlic salt, mixing well. Arrange salmon in one layer in a shallow container and cover with marinade. Marinate several hours, or overnight.

To make **Juniper Butter**, combine butter, parsley flakes, and juniper berries and heat until butter melts. Stir to combine.

To serve, sprinkle juniper berries and parsley flakes evenly over both sides of fish (1/4 teaspoon juniper berries and 1/16 teaspoon parsley per side) pressing into flesh. Grill fish 10 minutes on one side, basting with juniper butter. Turn over and grill 10 minutes on other side.

Brush with juniper butter before serving and garnish with parsley and lemon wheel.

Note: Juniper berries available from gourmet grocery stores.

MAKES 6 SERVINGS
Photograph, Page 24

"The appetite grows by eating."
FRANCOIS RABELAIS

VEGETABLES · BREADS

DAILEY'S

17 International Boulevard NE, Atlanta, GA 30303; (404) 681-3303.

Dailey's is an amiable sort of place. Located in the heart of downtown Atlanta's shopping and hotel district, this handsomely restored brick warehouse, with its skylights, wide floorboards, antique carousel horses, and baskets of green plants, lures throngs of Peachtree Center business people, tourists, and conventioneers. Atlantans come down for lunch, to enjoy the American/continental fare in the evenings, and to linger over cocktails and wine while talented young singers perform in the lounge.

STUFFED ARTICHOKES

6 large artichokes
$1/2$ cup lemon juice
3 to 5 cloves garlic
1 large bunch fresh parsley,
    minced
1 pound mushrooms, sliced
$1/2$ cup butter
2 tablespoons peanut oil
1 cup Parmesan cheese, grated
1 cup bread crumbs
1 teaspoon salt
$1/2$ teaspoon black pepper
2 tablespoons butter, melted
Garnish: 3 teaspoons paprika and
    6 lemon wedges

Add lemon juice to water and boil artichokes in enough water to cover for 35 to 45 minutes until tender. Immerse artichokes in ice water to stop cooking. Drain immediately.

Finely mince garlic, parsley, and slice mushrooms. Remove stalks from bottom of artichokes and roughly chop.

Heat butter and oil in large skillet and saute garlic, parsley, mushrooms, and artichoke stalks until tender. Combine with cheese, bread crumbs, and seasonings, mixing well. (Add more oil if mixture seems dry.)

Open artichokes, remove chokes ensuring all thistle is removed, and stuff the center of each with about $3/4$ cup stuffing.

Heat oven to 375 degrees F. and bake 7 to 10 minutes to heat through.

Drizzle melted butter over tops. Sprinkle $1/2$ teaspoon paprika over each artichoke and serve with lemon wedge.

MAKES 6 SERVINGS

LICKSKILLET FARM

Roswell and Rockmill Rds., Roswell, GA 30076; (404) 475-6484.

An evening at Lickskillet Farm removes you from the city's maddening rush, into the quiet and serenity of an elegant country house. The antebellum Lickskillet Farm house, set above a picturesque gazebo and stream, provides a memorable setting for a four-course meal of homemade soup, cracklin' bread, fresh vegetables, dessert, and an entree selection of steaks, frog legs, lobster tails, seafoods and chicken either Southern-fried or continental with wine sauce.

LICKSKILLET COUNTRY CABBAGE

1 medium head cabbage,
   shredded
1 medium onion, chopped
2 green peppers, chopped
1 quart water
Pinch of baking soda
1 (29-ounce) can tomatoes
1 tablespoon caraway seeds
Salt and pepper to taste

Mix cabbage, onion, and peppers together. Place in large pan with water, add soda, tomatoes, caraway seeds, and salt and pepper to taste. Bring all ingredients to boil and simmer approximately 1 hour.

MAKES 4 TO 6 SERVINGS

MARY MAC'S TEA ROOM

224 Ponce de Leon Ave., Atlanta, GA 30308; (404) 875-4337.

Ask a native Atlantan directions to the best Southern homecooking in town, and he'll point you toward Mary Mac's. This labyrinth of bustling dining rooms has been serving exquisite fried chicken, fresh vegetables, home-baked breads and desserts for more than 50 years. At lunch, the rooms are filled with business people and students from local colleges. At night, family groups and couples drop in to enjoy a great dinner for an astonishingly low price.

FRESH SOUTHERN TURNIP GREENS

3 pounds turnip greens with roots
2 ounces fatback (see Note)
Chicken broth
1 teaspoon salt
White pepper and salt
Chicken fat
Hot pepper sauce, optional

Select crisp, young greens without yellow or insect-bitten leaves. Roots should be no bigger than an orange, and white, not yellow.

Cut off the roots, peel, cube, and place in clear water, to be added to the greens for the last 20 to 30 minutes of cooking.

Pick over the leaves, discarding any withered or yellow ones and any large tough stalks. Wash them through several waters until the water is perfectly clear.

In a heavy pot, place a piece of fatback that has been scored or sliced so it will cook more quickly. Cover over about 1 inch with water and boil 30 minutes. Add washed greens and enough chicken broth to cover. Add 1 teaspoon salt. Simmer slowly in covered pan 1 hour. Do not allow to boil dry. Add more water and/or chicken broth if necessary. Add white turnip roots.

When greens are almost as tender as spinach, remove from pot, cut in small pieces, and return to pot. Taste and season with salt, white pepper, chicken fat, and hot pepper sauce, if desired. Discard fatback. These greens are even better when warmed over. Serve with hot corn bread.

Note: the strip of fat from the back of a hog, cured by drying and salting.

MAKES 4 SERVINGS.
Photograph, Page 21

PLANTATION ROOM

Callaway Gardens, Pine Mountain, Georgia 31822; (404) 663-2281.

One of America's most unique and beautiful resorts, Callaway Gardens was founded by the late Cason J. Callaway as a place where all people could find a measure of tranquility. Within this preserve, guests wander through 13 miles of scenic drives, nature trails, woodlands, lakes, and gardens that bloom in every season. Dining ranges from bountiful Southern-style buffets, American and continental gourmet cuisine, and hearty steaks and ribs. Before or after dinner, enjoy your favorite libation in the lounge, with live entertainment.

CALLAWAY GARDEN'S CARROT SOUFFLE

3 pounds carrots, cooked and
*   mashed*
1/3 cup butter
Pinch salt
1/3 cup milk
Sugar to taste
Vanilla to taste
1/2 teaspoon cinnamon
Pinch nutmeg
2 tablespoons flour
2 eggs, beaten

Blend mashed carrots with butter, salt, milk, sugar, and seasonings. Add flour and blend until smooth. Fold in beaten eggs. Pour mixture into buttered baking dish. Bake at 350 degrees F. for 30 to 40 minutes or until browned evenly.

MAKES 6 SERVINGS
Photograph, Page 17

UNICOI STATE PARK

Highway 356, Helen, GA 30545; (404) 878-2201.

In the green bower of the northeast Georgia mountains, Unicoi State Park is a 1023-acre retreat whose recreational opportunities include a lake for swimming, boating, and fishing; the Chattahoochee National Forest to hike in; folk culture programs; campgrounds; and craft shops. Guests in the wooden, country-rustic Unicoi Lodge, and hungry folks who just drop by, enjoy fresh mountain trout, vegetables, cobblers, and other home-cooked specialties. The Lodge is a beautiful destination any season.

UNICOI'S SQUASH CASSEROLE

2¹/₂ pounds yellow squash
1 medium onion, finely chopped
2¹/₂ slices white bread, crusts
 removed
¹/₂ cup butter or margarine,
 melted
1 cup seasoned croutons
1 cup milk
¹/₂ teaspoon Worcestershire sauce
Dash Tabasco sauce
1 clove garlic, pressed
2 eggs, slightly beaten
1 cup sharp Cheddar cheese,
 shredded
¹/₄ teaspoon salt
Paprika

Cut squash into quarter-inch slices. Place in saucepan with chopped onions. Cover with salted water and boil until onion is transparent. Drain and let cool.

Place sliced bread in oven. Turn to 350 degrees F., leave slices in oven approximately 4 to 5 minutes until slightly dry. Remove slices and cut into half-inch squares. Add to squash.

Melt butter in saucepan over low heat. Pour half into squash and bread mixture and stir thoroughly.

Add seasoned croutons to remaining butter, stir thoroughly, and set aside.

Add all other ingredients, except croutons and paprika, to squash. Turn into buttered baking dish. Mixture should be 2- to 3-inches deep with at least 1 inch left for rising.

Cover with buttered seasoned croutons, dust lightly with paprika, and bake at 350 degrees F. for about 30 minutes or until croutons are browned.

MAKES 8 SERVINGS

HERREN'S

84 Luckie St. NE, Atlanta, GA 30303; (404) 524-4709.

Atlantans have relied on Herren's cheerful service and delicious seafoods and steaks since 1934, when prizefighter "Red" Herren opened the doors downtown on Luckie Street. Through the years, the Negri family has expanded the menu, while never losing Herren's original personal touch. Located in the rejuvenating Fairlie-Poplar area, Herren's is still where Atlantans and visitors come for Maine lobster, London broil, and other favorites served in charming Williamsburg-style dining rooms enhanced by original art works.

SWEET ROLLS FROM HERREN'S

1 cup milk
1/4 cup butter
1/4 cup sugar
1 1/4 teaspoons salt
2 packages dry yeast
1/4 cup warm water
4 cups flour, sifted
Cinnamon-sugar mixture (2 cups
    sugar and 4 tablespoons
    cinnamon)
Melted butter

In a heavy saucepan boil the milk. Add butter, sugar, and salt. Cool. Soften yeast in water and stir into first mixture. Add flour, about half at a time, and beat well. Turn out on a floured board, allow to sit for 15 minutes, then knead until smooth.

Place dough in buttered bowl, cover with a cloth, and let rise in warm place until double in size. Roll out dough on a floured board to about one quarter-inch thick and cut into rough 8-inch squares.

Working with one square at a time, brush melted butter and sprinkle cinnamon-sugar mixture generously over entire surface. Starting at one side of the square roll up into a tube. Continue rolling tube back and forth until it is 12 to 16 inches long. Cut tube into wheels approximately one-half inch wide and place flat in pan that has been brushed with melted butter and sprinkled thoroughly with cinnamon-sugar mixture.

Place sweet rolls in pan (see Note) so that they touch, but do not over pack. Brush top with butter and sprinkle more cinnamon-sugar mixture generously over top. Let stand at room temperature for 1 hour.

Bake at 350 degrees F. for 18 to 20 minutes. Cover with aluminum foil and refrigerate. Allow 30 minutes to bring back to room temperature after removing from refrigerator.

Note: As this recipe makes 60 to 80 sweet rolls, use three or four small (6- to 8-inch) aluminum pans. This will allow you to stagger cooking during your dinner or leave to bake for breakfast.

MAKES ABOUT 60 ROLLS

MARY MAC'S TEA ROOM

228 Ponce de Leon Ave., NE, Atlanta, GA 30308; (404) 876-6604.

Landmarks come and go, but happily for those who appreciate southern homecooking at its delectable best, Mary Mac's just keeps on keeping on. After more than 25 years, this venerable Atlanta institution is still renowned for its delicious fried chicken, slowly-simmered vegetables, home-baked breads, and desserts. You write out your own order, and in a jiffy steaming bowls and platters will be set before your wondering eyes. You can even sip a cocktail and wine with your collard greens and country fried steak.

CORN BREAD MUFFINS

1 pound white corn meal
1 cup plain flour
2 tablespoons sugar
2 tablespoons baking powder
1/2 teaspoon baking soda
4 teaspoons salt
2 eggs
3 1/3 cups buttermilk
4 tablespoons lard, melted

Mix together corn meal, flour, sugar, baking powder, baking soda, and salt.
Beat eggs. Add buttermilk and melted lard.
Mix buttermilk mixture into corn meal mixture. Grease muffin tin well. Fill each cup two-thirds full with corn bread mixture.
Bake in hot oven at 400 to 450 degrees F. until brown on top, about 15 to 20 minutes.
MAKES 12 to 15 MUFFINS
Photograph, Page 21

THEODORE'S

Holiday Inn Downtown, 121 West Boundary St., Savannah, GA 31402; (912) 236-1355.

Guests at the Holiday Inn may unwind with live entertainment and dancing in the lounges, and enjoy local seafoods, steaks, and southern favorites with their favorite wines and cocktails in Theodore's dining room. Only a few blocks from the center of downtown Savannah's lovely historic homes and park-like squares, the Holiday Inn Downtown offers guests 210 beautifully furnished and air-conditioned rooms, and a swimming pool for relaxation after a busy day's sightseeing.

OLD-FASHIONED BUTTERMILK BISCUITS

3 cups self-rising flour
3 tablespoons shortening
1 teaspoon baking powder
1 tablespoon sugar
1 cup buttermilk
Melted butter

Combine flour, shortening, baking powder, and sugar together and blend until coarse in texture. Add buttermilk and knead until smooth. Roll out on flat, floured surface and cut with biscuit cutter.
Bake at 400 degrees F. for 10 to 12 minutes or until brown. Brush with melted butter.
MAKES 12 BISCUITS

"There is no spectacle on earth more appealing than that of a beautiful woman in the act of cooking dinner for someone she loves."

THOMAS WOLFE, *THE WEB AND THE ROCK*

DESSERTS · PASTRIES · BEVERAGES

THE ABBEY

163 Ponce de Leon Ave., NE, Atlanta, GA 30308; (404) 876-8532.

The Abbey is a haven for sybarites who revere the most exquisite delicacies, accompanied by the finest wines. Guests in this former church, now an award-winning, four-star restaurant, sit under stained-glass windows and a soaring vaulted ceiling. Candlelight flickers on every table, and the soothing music of a harpist enhances the magical spell. Servers, in monks' habits, present a feast of classical French cuisine that will be remembered long after the evening is over.

FROZEN GRAND MARNIER SOUFFLE

³/₄ cup sugar
7 egg yolks
3 tablespoons Grand Marnier
2 tablespoons cognac
¹/₄ cup frozen orange juice
    concentrate
2 cups heavy cream, chilled
Garnish: whipped cream and
    cherry

Using an electric mixer, beat sugar and egg yolks at high speed until light and fluffy. At low speed, add Grand Marnier, cognac, and frozen orange juice concentrate.

Chill another bowl, and whip cream at medium speed until soft, but not stiff.

With a wooden spoon or rubber spatula, fold the two mixtures together, until the whipped cream is completely incorporated.

Put into individual glasses or a large souffle dish with a three-inch band of wax paper around the edge, two inches extending above the top. (Can be held together with tape.) Freeze overnight.

Remove wax paper, if frozen in a souffle dish, and garnish with additional whipped cream and a cherry.

MAKES 12 (4-OUNCE) SERVINGS

AUNT FANNY'S CABIN

375 Campbell Rd., Smyrna, GA 30081; (404) 436-9026.

The nucleus of this suburban Atlanta culinary landmark was once an actual slave cabin. Today, Aunt Fanny's is the place where Atlantans and out-of-towners repair for the genuine Southern treatment. In an atmosphere of ceiling fans, checkered tablecloths, and Old South entertainment, youngsters recite the menu, and diners savor some of the world's finest fried chicken, Smithfield ham, Georgia mountain trout, steaks, and other entrees accompanied by a rainbow of slowly-simmered vegetables, cornbread, and cobbler.

APPLE COBBLER

8 cooking apples or enough to
   make 8 cups
1 cup water
1 cup sugar (or more for
   tart apples)
Pinch nutmeg
1 tablespoon butter, melted
1 tablespoon cornstarch
$1/2$ cup water
2 cups self-rising flour, sifted
4 tablespoons sugar
3 teaspoons baking powder
$1/2$ cup shortening
Ice water

Peel, core, and slice apples into $1/4$-inch thick pieces. Place in pot with 1 cup water, bring to boil, then simmer until tender but still firm. Drain water. Mix in sugar, nutmeg, and butter. Mix cornstarch with $1/2$ cup water and add to apple mixture. Place in 9-inch-square baking dish.

Mix flour, sugar, baking powder, and lard. Rub with your hands until it forms fine crumbs. Sprinkle with ice water and mix until it holds together and forms a dough.

Roll out as thin as possible for pie crust. Cover apples with crust.

Bake at 350 degrees F. for about 45 minutes. Cut into squares and serve warm with cream.

Individual apple cobblers may also be made.

MAKES 6 TO 8 SERVINGS

THE BOULEVARD RESTAURANT

Radisson Inn Atlanta, I-285 North at Chamblee-Dunwoody Rd., Atlanta, GA 30338; (404) 394-5000.

The Radisson Inn is a multi-faceted suburban resort on Atlanta's affluent northeast side. Guests are only minutes from regional shopping malls, restaurants, and nightclubs, and a half hour or less from downtown or Stone Mountain. Yet, they have the luxury of six tennis courts, two swimming pools, and a complete health club. Dining is first-class in the Radisson's Boulevard Restaurant, which features the finest steaks, seafoods, classical continental cuisine, elegant desserts, cocktails, and wines.

GRASSHOPPER PIE

1 (¹/₄-ounce) package plain gelatin
1 cup half-and-half cream
1 cup sugar
8 egg yolks
¹/₂ cup Creme de Cocoa (white)
¹/₂ cup Creme de Menthe (green)
2 cups heavy cream
2 (10-inch) baked pie shells
Garnish: whipped cream and
    shaved chocolate

Sprinkle gelatin over half-and-half cream and allow to soak for 5 minutes. Then heat in top of double boiler to dissolve gelatin.

Blend sugar with egg yolks, and then add the hot cream with gelatin. Return mixture to double boiler and heat until thick, stirring constantly. Add Creme de Cocoa and Creme de Menthe. Remove from heat, chill, but do not let set.

Whip cream until stiff and fold into the chilled mixture. Pour into prebaked pie shells and chill until set.

Garnish with whipped cream and shaved chocolate.

MAKES 2 (10-INCH) PIES
Photograph, Page 17

CALVERT'S

Surrey Shopping Center, 475 Highland Ave., Augusta, GA 30909; (404) 738-4514.

This beautiful, sophisticated restaurant is just the place for an elegant dinner and cocktails after an exciting day at the Masters Golf Tournament, or after a tour of Augusta's many lovely homes and historic buildings, or when you are in the mood for something special. The decor is elegant, the service friendly and discreet. The menu offers a tempting selection of your favorite American dishes and many continental surprises. Bananas Foster and other delectable desserts top off a memorable luncheon or dinner.

CHOCOLATE ALMOND MOUSSE TORTE

$1^1/2$ cups chocolate wafer crumbs
$1^1/2$ cups toasted almonds, crushed
$^1/2$ cup unsalted butter, melted
1 pound semi-sweet chocolate
2 eggs
4 egg yolks
$^1/4$ cup Kahlua
2 cups whipping cream
6 tablespoons powdered sugar
4 egg whites, room temperture
2 cups whipping cream for topping
Sugar
$^1/2$ cup toasted almonds for topping

To make crust, combine crumbs, crushed almonds, and butter. Line bottom and sides of 10-inch springform pan.
Refrigerate 30 minutes or chill in freezer.
For filling: Soften chocolate in top of double boiler over simmering water. Let cool to lukewarm (95 degrees F.). Add whole eggs and mix well. Add yolks and Kahlua and mix until thoroughly blended.
Whip cream with powdered sugar until soft peaks form. Beat egg whites until stiff but not dry. Stir $^1/4$ cup cream and half egg whites into chocolate mixture to lighten. Fold in $1^3/4$ cups cream and remaining egg whites until completely incorporated. Turn into crust and chill at least 6 hours or, preferably, overnight.
For assembly: Whip remaining 2 cups cream with sugar to taste until quite stiff. Loosen crust on all sides using knife. Remove springform. Spread half cream over top of torte and evenly sprinkle with toasted almonds. Pipe remaining cream around outer top edge of torte. Use fishing line to cut wedges of torte.
MAKES 8 TO 10 SERVINGS

CARBO'S CAFE

3717 Roswell Rd., NW, Atlanta, GA 30342; (404) 231-4433.

One of Northside Atlanta's most popular continental cafes, Carbo's excels in small, personal touches. Fresh roses adorn the beautifully set tables — the crystal and china were selected by the owners with great care. Art works grace the walls. Pleasant piano music relaxes you, and sets the proper mood for an evening of excellent continental cuisine. A wonderful selection of special coffees is available for after dinner. Put it all together, and you have a lovely place to enjoy a quiet dinner with someone special.

BRANDIED PUMPKIN CHEESECAKE

2 cups graham cracker crumbs
1 tablespoon sugar
1/2 teaspoon cinnamon
10 tablespoons melted butter
4 (8-ounce) packages
*   cream cheese*
1 pound light brown sugar
1 (1-pound 14-ounce) can
*   solid-pack pumpkin*
8 large eggs, room temperature
2 teaspoons cinnamon
1 teaspoon ginger
1/2 teaspoon nutmeg
2 tablespoons flour
1/4 cup brandy
1/4 cup cream
Garnish: whipped cream

Mix together graham cracker crumbs, sugar, 1/2 teaspoon cinnamon, and melted butter. Press into bottom of a 9-inch springform pan.
Beat cream cheese well. Beat in brown sugar. Beat in pumpkin, scrape down bowl, and beat again. Lower speed and add eggs, one at a time. Add remaining cinnamon, ginger, nutmeg, and flour. Then add cream and brandy.
Pour into springform pan. Place pan in shallow water bath (larger pan with water in). Bake in preheated oven at 350 degrees F. for 2 hours. Remove from oven. Chill completely. Remove from pan, decorate with whipped cream, and serve.
MAKES 1 (9-INCH) CHEESECAKE, 12 SERVINGS
Photograph, Page 22

THE COACH AND SIX RESTAURANT

1776 Peachtree St., NW, Atlanta, GA 30309; (404) 872-6666.

The Coach and Six has been an Atlanta tradition since 1962, when New Yorkers Hank and Beverlee Soloff opened their sophisticated dining rooms on Peachtree Street. Regular patrons swear allegiance to the Coach's prime-aged Colorado beef, along with other dishes that have a sterling reputation for consistency, while the black bean soup is nationally famous. The professional service is as always among the city's most knowledgeable. Celebrities and friends are enshrined on a mural in the bar.

COACH AND SIX "20TH" ANNIVERSARY TORTE

2 egg whites
1¹/₂ tablespoons sugar
1¹/₂ tablespoons pecans, finely chopped
2 tablespoons flour
1 tablespoon melted butter
1 quart whipping cream with sugar to taste
¹/₂ teaspoon vanilla
1 (10-inch-round, ¹/₄-inch thick) sponge cake (available from bakery, or use your favorite recipe)
¹/₂ tablespoon cherry brandy
2 cups (about) cinnamon sugar
³/₄ cup melted semi-sweet chocolate, or any dark chocolate
Granulated sugar
Cocoa powder and coconut, finely grated
2 cups canned, pitted Bing cherries
Simple syrup as needed (see Glossary)
Cinnamon to taste

Beat egg whites with half sugar until stiff. Add pecans, rest of sugar and flour. Mix well. Add melted butter last.

Grease and flour 2 cookie sheets. Spread mixture ¹/₈-inch thick evenly over each. Bake in a preheated 350-degree-F. oven for 8 to 10 minutes, until light brown. Remove and let cool. Whip cream with sugar to taste and add vanilla. On 1 round plate, at least 14 inches in diameter, place dabs of whipped cream in the middle to keep torte in place. Place sponge cake in middle of plate. Sprinkle cake with cherry brandy. Cover evenly with a ¹/₄-inch layer of whipped cream, then with broken pieces of pecan crust. Sprinkle with cinnamon sugar. Repeat whipped cream, pecan crust, and cinnamon sugar layers three more times. Over fourth layer, put ¹/₄-inch of cream and also evenly cover sides.

Combine remaining whipped cream with ¹/₄-cup of chocolate. Form into about 24 balls and refrigerate. When chilled and firm, dip balls into remaining melted chocolate and then roll in granulated sugar. Refrigerate until chocolate hardens. Then roll some in cocoa powder or some in coconut as desired. Dust whole torte with cocoa powder if desired.

Mark 12 even slices on top of torte. Decorate each marked slice with chocolate and/or coconut balls.

Combine cherries and some simple syrup with cinnamon to taste. Surround each torte with cherries.

Freeze for 1¹/₂ to 2 hours before slicing and serving.

MAKES 1 TORTE, 12 SERVINGS

DAILEY'S

17 International Boulevard NE, Atlanta, GA 30303; (404) 681-3303.

Join the friendly crew at Dailey's for a hamburger, gourmet sandwich or salad in the lounge. Or, take a walk up the grand staircase and into a charming setting of natural brick walls, antiques, and green plants. Go deluxe all the way with the Peasant Group's acclaimed American and international seafoods, veal, beef, and pork creations, topped off by some of the most luscious desserts this side of Old Vienna. In the evenings, the downstairs lounge is a showcase for talented young singers and musicians.

RAISIN CREAM CHEESE STRUDEL

¹/₂ cup ground walnuts
3 tablespoons unseasoned
  bread crumbs
¹/₂ cup raisins
3 cups hot water
12 ounces cream cheese, softened
2 tablespoons unsalted butter,
  softened
¹/₂ cup sugar
1 egg
1 teaspoon fresh lemon juice
1 teaspoon pure vanilla extract
5 sheets phyllo dough
  (see Glossary)
¹/₄ pound unsalted butter, melted
2 tablespoons powdered sugar

Preheat oven to 375 degrees F. Line cookie sheet with parchment paper.

Combine walnuts and bread crumbs in small bowl. Set aside. Combine raisins and hot water in another small bowl and set aside.

Beat cream cheese and 2 tablespoons butter until soft. Add sugar and beat until there are no lumps. Add egg, lemon juice, and vanilla extract. Stir until smooth.

Drain water from raisins and add raisins to cheese filling.

Place 1 sheet of phyllo dough on pastry cloth or cloth napkin. Brush with melted butter. Repeat until you have 5 stacked sheets of phyllo, each brushed with butter.

Sprinkle dough with walnut-crumb mixture. Spoon filling along long side of dough. Roll up tightly. Place on prepared pan, seam side down. Brush with butter.

Bake at 375 degrees F. for 25 to 30 minutes or until golden brown. When cool, sprinkle with powdered sugar. Cut diagonally.

MAKES 6 SERVINGS
Photograph, Page 17

DANTE'S DOWN THE HATCH

3380 Peachtree Rd., NE, Atlanta, GA 30326; (404) 266-1600.

In the heart of landlocked Atlanta, guests at Dante's Down the Hatch sail blissfully away from mundane cares in the facsimile of an 18th-century brigantine, handsomely outfitted with masts, riggings, and 200-year-old hand-stitched sails. "Passengers" may also enjoy the comforts of the lighthouse balcony, captain's table, or private dining rooms while enjoying great jazz, folk music, fondues, cheese, and wines and cocktails. "Captain" Dante Stephensen is always on hand to greet and mingle with his guests.

CHOCOLATE FONDUE

1 1/2 to 2 cups half-and-half cream
6 to 8 (3-ounce) bars Toblerone
    chocolate (or comparable
    Dutch, Danish, or Swiss milk
    chocolate with almonds
    and honey)
Dash instant coffee
Dash cinnamon
2 teaspoons Cointreau or favorite
    liqueur

In top of double boiler over low heat, cover bottom of pan with cream. Add chocolate, breaking into small chunks. Melt chocolate, adding more cream as necessary, until mix is smooth. Do not scorch. Add coffee and cinnamon.

Simmer in top of double boiler for 6 to 8 hours adding cream as needed to keep it from getting too thick.

Pour Cointreau or other liqueur into bottom of ceramic pot, then pour in chocolate mixture. Serve hot in ceramic pot with candle under to keep warm.

Serve it with any of the following:

Fresh strawberries; fresh Hawaiian pineapple chunks; 1-inch banana slices; cantaloupe or honeydew melon cut into 1-inch pieces; seedless grapes; cherries, sliced peaches, blueberries (large), raspberries, sliced pears, tangerine sections, blackberries when in season; rum-soaked cake, angel food cake, or pound cake cut into 1-inch cubes; mandarin orange sections; small marshmallows.

MAKES 6 SERVINGS

HOLIDAY INN RESTAURANT

Holiday Inn — Waycross, Highways 1, 23 and 84, Waycross, GA 31501; (912) 283-4490.

The modern, 145-room Holiday Inn of Waycross is only seven miles from the entrance to the world-famous Okefenokee Swamp Park. After your visit to this "Land of Trembling Earth," you may relax in the Holiday Inn's landscaped courtyard with swimming pool and lighted putting green. Breakfast, lunch, and dinner, featuring American and continental favorites, are served in the pleasant contemporary dining room. The lounge offers wines and your favorite libations.

EMMA LEE'S PECAN CHIFFON PIE

4 eggs, separated
$^1/_4$ teaspoon salt
1 cup sugar
1 cup milk
1 envelope plain gelatin
$^1/_4$ cup cold water
1 teaspoon vanilla extract
1 cup pecans, chopped
   and toasted
1 (9-inch) baked pie shell
Whipped cream with sugar and
   vanilla to taste for topping

Beat egg yolks, place in pan with salt and half sugar. In separate pan heat milk and then pour over egg mixture, bring to boil over low heat and cook until thickened.

Remove from stove and while still hot stir in gelatin dissolved in water. (Do not let gelatin stand.) Add vanilla, and then cool custard completely.

Beat egg whites until stiff, adding remaining sugar. Fold into cool custard mixture. Gradually add pecans.

Put into baked pie shell and refrigerate. After pie sets, add whipped cream topping and refrigerate until serving time.

Variations: Substitute toasted almonds and almond flavoring or toasted coconut and coconut flavoring for vanilla and pecans.

MAKES 8 SERVINGS

INTERNATIONAL FOOD WORKS

Georgia-Pacific Center, 133 Peachtree St., NE, Atlanta, GA 30303; (404) 529-9416.

Since the opening of the International Food Works, a most pleasant self-service restaurant in Georgia-Pacific Corporation's 52-story skyscraper, downtown luncheon habits have never been the same. Like a culinary World's Fair, diners have a choice of exciting cuisines — Chinese, Mexican, New York deli sandwiches and bagels, fresh seafoods, hamburgers, European specialties, homemade ice creams and desserts — in a busy, modern setting. You can even "take out" a selection of breakfast, lunch, and snack items.

TORTE AU FROMAGE BLANC

3 ¼ cups granulated sugar
5 cups water
8 egg yolks, beaten
1 ounce (4 packages) plain gelatin
1 quart simple syrup (4 cups
    water, 2 cups granulated sugar)
4 (8-ounce) packages
    cream cheese
¼ cup grapefruit juice
1 quart whipping cream
1 (9-inch) white layer cake from
    your favorite recipe or
    from bakery

Cook sugar and water to soft ball stage. Combine with egg yolks, and mix until cool. Mix gelatin with simple syrup, warm to dissolve gelatin. Soften cream cheese. Combine sugar and yolks mixture and gelatin mixture. Add grapefruit juice.

Whip cream and fold in cream cheese, sugar and yolks, gelatin, and grapefruit juice.

Line 9-inch springform pan with layer of white cake. Fold mixture into pan. Let stand in refrigerator overnight before serving.

MAKES 8 TO 10 SERVINGS
Photograph, Page 22

LAPRADE'S RESTAURANT, CABINS & MARINA

Route 1, Highway 197 N, Clarkesville, GA 30523; (404) 947-3312.

LaPrade's has nestled by the shores of Lake Burton, in the northeast Georgia mountains, since the 1920s. In a setting reminiscent of a camp dining hall, guests enjoy delicious family-style meals that feature homemade sausage and hot biscuits for breakfast, chicken and dumplings at lunch, and fried chicken and all the accessories at dinner, along with relaxed conversation. All this, and the lake is fairly jumping with fish.

BAKED APPLES

12 Staymen apples or
    cooking apples
1$^1/_2$ cups sugar
$^1/_2$ cup light brown sugar
$^3/_4$ teaspoon cinnamon
$^3/_4$ teaspoon nutmeg
$^3/_4$ teaspoon allspice
$^3/_4$ teaspoon crushed cardamon
    or ginger
$^1/_4$ cup butter
Marshmallow cream or whipped
    cream to top

Core apples and cut into quarters. Place in baking dish. Combine sugars and sprinkle over apples. Then combine spices and sprinkle over apples, also. Cut butter into 12 slices and distribute on top of apples.

Bake at 350 degrees F. for approximately 30 minutes, or until apples are soft.

For extra effect top with either marshmallow cream or whipped cream.

MAKES 6 SERVINGS

LE PAPILLON RESTAURANT

785 Edgewood Ave., Atlanta, GA 30307; (404) 688-2172.

In the heart of Atlanta's beautifully restored Inman Park Victorian neighborhood, only a mile and a half from downtown, Le Papillon blends the charms of a 19th-century setting with fine French provincial cuisine in small, intimate dining rooms. Entrees include imaginative and creative ways with trout, shellfish, meats, and poultry. Home-baked breads and desserts are special treats, and Le Papillon's wine list includes a wide range of French, Italian, and California vintages, all moderately priced.

BITTERSWEET FRENCH CHOCOLATE CAKE

4 large eggs, separated (room
    temperature)
²/₃ cup sugar
¹/₄ cup coffee, strong
3 squares (3 ounces)
    unsweetened baking chocolate
2 tablespoons butter
¹/₃ cup sugar
¹/₂ cup butter
Pinch salt
Pinch cream of tartar
2 tablespoons sugar
³/₄ cup cornstarch

Apricot Filling
1 (1-pound) can apricots
¹/₃ cup sugar
Juice and grated rind of
    1 lemon
1 tablespoon brandy

Butter Cream Frosting
¹/₄ cup coffee
2 squares unsweetened chocolate
2 tablespoons butter
¹/₃ cup sugar
³/₄ cup butter, soft
2 egg yolks
²/₃ cup confectioners sugar
Grated rind of 1 orange
2 tablespoons Grand Marnier

Chopped almonds to decorate

Preheat oven to 350 degrees F.
Cake: In large bowl beat yolks, gradually adding sugar. In mixer beat until stiff and smooth. Grease 2 round 8-inch by 1¹/₂-inch deep cake pans with butter. Line the bottom with buttered wax paper. Flour lightly, knocking out excess. Put coffee in saucepan over low heat. Add chocolate and butter to melt. Add sugar and mix until smooth. Beat in ¹/₂ cup butter. Add chocolate mixture to yolk mixture. In a separate bowl beat egg whites until frothy. Add pinches of salt and cream of tartar. Beat until soft peaks form. Add 2 tablespoons sugar, beat until stiff peaks form. Stir quarter of whites into chocolate mixture to lighten. Add rest of whites on top and fold in gently, but rapidly, sifting on the cornstarch in 4 batches. Pour into pans and bake for exactly 15 minutes. Centers should remain soft. Remove, cool, and then chill in pans. **Apricot Filling:** Drain juice from apricot can into saucepan. Stir in sugar and boil down rapidly to thicken. Chop apricots to desired consistency. Add them with juice and grated lemon rind to thickened juices and bring back to boil. Remove from heat, add brandy. Chill. **Butter Cream Frosting:** Put coffee, chocolate, and butter in top of double boiler to melt. Add sugar, beat until smooth. Remove from heat, beat in butter. In separate bowl beat yolks with confectioners sugar, add orange rind and Grand Marnier. Mix into chocolate butter mixture until smooth. Chill to spreading consistency.
To assemble: Warm cake pans slightly to remove chilled layers. Put apricot filling between two layers. Spread chocolate butter cream on top and sides. Brush chopped almonds on sides only and chill until ready to serve. MAKES 8 TO 10 SERVINGS

THE LOBBY LOUNGE

Omni International Hotel, One Omni International, Atlanta, GA 30335; (404) 659-0000.

The Omni International Hotel's Lobby Cocktail Lounge is a contemporary and elegant retreat for cocktails, specialty desserts, and hors d'oeuvres. Elevated seating arrangements create intimate spaces for conversation and relaxation, while the location also makes it an intriguing spot for people-watching. The mood is enhanced by a pleasant and attentive staff, and two highly visible and decorative food and beverage displays whet the appetite, where the emphasis is placed on the "After 8" experience, one not easily forgotten.

AMARETTO COCONUT MOUSSE

1/4 cup Amaretto liqueur
2 teaspoons gelatin
1 1/2 cups whipping cream
1 cup sugar
1/2 cup sour cream
3/4 cup toasted, finely shredded coconut
Shaved chocolate to top

In a saucepan heat liqueur and gelatin until just warm.
Whip cream until stiff, add sugar and sour cream.
Fold in the liqueur and gelatin mix. Then fold in coconut.
Fill 4 (10-ounce) glasses. Chill for one hour.
To serve top with shaved chocolate.
MAKES 4 SERVINGS

THE LOBBY LOUNGE

Omni International Hotel, One Omni International, Atlanta, GA 30335; (404) 659-0000.

Since its opening in 1975, the Omni International Hotel has enjoyed an enviable reputation as one of Atlanta's most elegant and continental hotels. Visitors from all over the world have returned home praising the hotel's beautiful guestrooms, fine cuisine and service. The Lobby Lounge is a memorable part of any visit. In the air of an enclosed sidewalk cafe, guests have a choice of cocktails, hors d'oeuvres and splendid desserts. It's a lovely place to meet friends and unwind after a busy day.

KEY LIME PIE

7 tablespoons butter
5 tablespoons sugar
1 1/2 ounces ground almonds
1/2 ounce biscuit crumbs
1 egg yolk
1 1/8 cups cake flour
Dash cinnamon
Dash baking powder
1 pound 2 ounces sweetened
*   condensed milk*
5 egg yolks
1/2 cup freshly squeezed lime
*   juice*
1/4 cup sugar
Garnish: Whipping cream if
*   desired*

Quickly beat butter in mixer, add sugar, ground almonds, biscuit crumbs, egg yolks, flour, cinnamon, and baking powder until it forms a dough. Do not over beat. Roll out to quarter inch thick and line the bottom of a deep (10-inch) pie pan. Prebake at 375 degrees F. for 10 to 15 minutes or until set.

Mix together condensed milk, egg yolks, lime juice, and sugar. Pour into pie shell.

Bake at 375 degrees F. for 10 to 15 minutes, or until set.

MAKES 1 (10-INCH) PIE

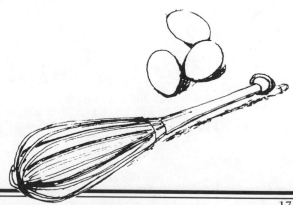

MICHELLE'S

Georgia-Pacific Center, 133 Peachtree St., NE, Atlanta, GA 30303; (404) 529-9400.

On the site of Loew's Grand Theater, where *Gone With the Wind* made its world premiere in 1939, there now stands a fine French restaurant. Michelle's, in the best European traditions, more than lives up to the hospitality and warmth of the Old South. Here, guests find a staff anxious to please, and cuisine and wines that would satisfy even the most discriminating palate in a setting elegant with marble, brass, and flowers. The lounge is in classical Art Deco-style and features live musical entertainment.

CHOCOLATE MOUSSE

8 ounces bitter chocolate
4 ounces sweet chocolate
14 egg yolks
1¹/₃ cups granulated sugar
1 quart whipping cream
10 egg whites
1¹/₂ teaspoons cream of tartar
2 tablespoons coffee liqueur
2 tablespoons brandy

Melt bitter chocolate with sweet chocolate.
Whip egg yolks with ¹/₂ cup plus 1 tablespoon sugar and put in bowl.
Whip cream and put in separate bowl.
Whip egg whites with ³/₄ cup sugar and cream of tartar.
Mix egg yolks with melted chocolate, coffee liqueur, brandy, whipped cream, and fold in egg whites.
Pour into individual glasses. Chill before serving.
MAKES 12 SERVINGS
Photograph, Page 24

THE PEASANT UPTOWN

Phipps Plaza Peachtree and Lenox Rds. NE, Atlanta, GA 30326; (404) 261-6341.

The Peasant Uptown is the perfect complement to the Phipps shopping adventure, Atlanta's most cosmopolitan shopping gallery, where Saks Fifth Avenue, Lord & Taylor, Gucci, Tiffany, and other glamorous names lend an air of New York and Beverly Hills. In this lovely greenhouse setting, you'll savor the Peasant Group's renowned American and continental cuisine at luncheon and dinner, set off by excellent cocktails and wine, and some of the most congenial service you'll find anywhere.

CHOCOLATE DIABLO

16 ounces semisweet chocolate
8 ounces unsweetened chocolate
³/₄ cup sugar
1 cup coffee
¹/₂ cup dark rum
1 cup unsalted butter, room
*   temperature*
3 cups heavy cream

Rum Cream
1 cup whipping cream
2 tablespoons confectioners sugar
1 tablespoon rum

Spray a bundt pan with Pam (or other food release spray).
Combine semisweet chocolate, unsweetened chocolate, sugar, coffee, and rum in double boiler over water.
Heat until chocolates melt, stirring often.
Remove from heat and cool for 15 minutes.
Cut butter into 1 inch cubes. Whisk butter into chocolate mixture until smooth. Let cool to room temperature.
Whip cream on high speed until it holds soft peaks. Gently, but thoroughly, fold whipped cream into chocolate mixture. Pour mixture into mold and refrigerate overnight.
Dip pan into warm water and unmold onto a large platter. Cut into eighths. Top each serving with Rum Cream.
To make Rum Cream, whip cream on high speed until it holds soft peaks. Add sugar and rum and whip a few seconds until combined. Serve over Chocolate Diablo.
MAKES 8 SERVINGS
Photograph, Page 22

PIRATES' HOUSE

20 East Broad St., Savannah, GA 31401; (912) 233-5757.

Sundays in Savannah are special, a time for quiet walks among the city's lovely old landmarks, followed by the bountiful Jazz Buffet Brunch at the famed Pirates' House. While the musicians beat out "Sweet Georgia Brown" and other favorites, guests are dazzled by a brunch spread that ranges from eggs to oysters, topped off with Pirates' House's thirty-six spectacular desserts. After brunch, take time to browse through the twenty-three dining rooms of this most unusual restaurant.

CHOCOLATE CHEESECAKE

20 thin chocolate wafers, crushed
¹/₄ cup melted butter or
  margarine
3 (8-ounce) packages cream
  cheese, softened
1 cup sugar
4 eggs, separated
1 teaspoon vanilla extract
1 (12-ounce) package semi-sweet
  chocolate chips, melted
1 cup (¹/₂ pint) heavy cream,
  whipped and sweetened
  to taste
Cocoa

To make crust, combine cookie crumbs and butter. (This can be done in a food processor.) Press onto bottom on a 10-inch springform pan. Preheat oven to 350 degrees F.

Beat cream cheese until smooth. Beat in half cup sugar, then egg yolks one at a time. Add vanilla extract and beat in melted chocolate. (This can all be done in a food processor.)

Beat egg whites with an electric mixer until they form soft peaks. Beat in remaining sugar, 1 tablespoon at a time. Continue beating until peaks are stiff but not dry.

Fold chocolate-cream cheese mixture into egg whites on low speed.

Pour into pan with crust and bake for 50 to 60 minutes until set. Cake will puff up and then sink and crack.

Cool on wire rack to room temperature, preferably overnight.

Serve with whipped cream and cocoa sifted on top. Or freeze the cheesecake for several hours then serve with whipped cream. Slice thin.

MAKES 8 to 10 SERVINGS

PLANTATION ROOM

Callaway Gardens, Pine Mountain, Georgia 31822; (404) 663-2281.

Callaway Gardens is truly a resort for all seasons. Sequestered in the rolling hills of west-central Georgia, this beautiful retreat has Florida sand beaches for summer swimming and boating. Fall brings chrysanthemums and brilliant fall foliage; winter, flaming holly berries; and in spring more than 600 varieties of azaleas. Guests at the Gardens Inn, and day visitors, enjoy delicious Southern, American/continental, and steaks-and-ribs cuisine in the Gardens' cheerful dining rooms.

CREME BRULEE

1 quart cream
$^1/_2$ cup sugar
$^1/_2$ teaspoon salt
8 egg yolks, beaten
1 teaspoon vanilla
Brown sugar

In the top of a double boiler, over hot water, scald cream with sugar and salt. Pour these ingredients slowly over beaten yolks. Add vanilla. Beat until well blended. Pour into a baking dish or individual molds and place in a pan of hot water. Bake at 325 degrees F. for 30 minutes, or until custard is set. Test with a silver knife. If custard does not adhere, it is ready to be removed from oven.

Chill, overnight if you wish.

Thirty minutes before serving, cover top with a good layer of sifted brown sugar. Place under broiler until sugar melts and carmelizes. *Watch carefully.* Chill until serving time.

MAKES 8 SERVINGS

Photograph, Page 24

THE PORTICO

Atlanta Marriott Hotel, Courtland St. at Int'l Blvd. NE, Atlanta, GA 30303; (404) 659-6500.

Even with downtown Atlanta's great restaurants, entertainment, and shopping a short walk away, it's small wonder that many Marriott guests can never seem to tear themselves away from the hotel. In the Portico you'll find a bright cheerful gathering place for local business people and visiting conventioneers and tourists alike, and as in all Marriott hotels, the service is excellent. This hotel boasts a New Orleans-style courtyard complete with an all-weather swimming pool. There is also a health club and outstanding evening entertainment.

BABA AU RUM

2 cups milk
2 ounces brewers yeast (cake yeast available at health food stores)
2 cups flour
1/3 cup sugar
12 large eggs
1 tablespoon salt
1 cup butter, melted
6 cups flour
Grated rind of 1 lemon

Warm milk and add to yeast. Mix in flour and allow to rise. Work in remaining ingredients. Put dough in greased bowl, cover with a damp cloth and allow to rise again.

Punch down. Divide into 4 equal parts and place each one in a greased or floured (or sprayed with nonstick vegetable oil) round forms, such as charlotte molds. Cover each with a damp cloth and allow to rise again.

Bake at 350 degrees F. for 30 to 35 minutes. Remove from forms and soak with Rum Syrup.

Rum Syrup

Heat 2 quarts water and 4 cups sugar together until sugar is dissolved, and liquid has consistency of maple syrup. Remove from heat and add juice from 1 lemon (2 tablespoons) and 1 whole cinnamon stick. Leave cinnamon stick in about half an hour. Remove. Add 1/2 cup rum. Stir and pour over babas.

Allow babas to soak several hours or overnight before serving.

MAKES 4 BABAS

THE PUBLIC HOUSE

607 Atlanta St., Roswell, GA 30075; (404) 992-4646.

In days of yore, a public house was a roadside inn, where the spirits of road-weary travelers were uplifted by hearty food and drink partaken in an aura of relaxed camaraderie. This Public House, facing Roswell's historic Town Square, reinvokes the age-old tradition of hospitality in its large, inviting dining rooms, furnished with paintings, antiques, and china. The Public House menu of innovative American and international dishes, cocktails and wines will inspire you to return again and again.

KAHLUA CHEESECAKE

¹/₂ cup butter
2 cups graham cracker crumbs
6 (8-ounce) packages
*   cream cheese*
3 cups sugar
¹/₄ cup cocoa
6 extra-large eggs
¹/₄ cup Kahlua
5 cups whipped cream
5 teaspoons chocolate shavings

Line bottom of (10-by 3-inch) cheesecake pan (not a springform pan) with parchment paper. Preheat oven to 350 degrees F.

Melt butter and combine with graham cracker crumbs. Pat into prepared pan and bake at 350 degrees F. for 10 minutes. Remove from oven and set aside.

Beat cream cheese in electric mixer until soft. Sift sugar and cocoa together. Add to cream cheese and beat until no lumps of cream cheese remain. Scrape bowl often. Add eggs and Kahlua and stir to combine. (See Note).

Pour batter into pan with graham cracker base. Place pan in roasting pan filled with 1 inch water. Bake cheesecake in "water-bath" at 350 degrees F. for 3 hours. Refrigerate overnight.

To remove cake from pan, dip pan in large pan filled with hot water for 15 seconds. Invert onto a large dish and rap gently until cake slides out of pan. Invert, right side up, onto serving dish.

Top each portion with half a cup whipped cream and half a teaspoon chocolate shavings.

Note: You may add 1 cup of chocolate chips to cream cheese mixture if desired.

MAKES 1 (10-INCH) CAKE, 10 SERVINGS
Photograph, Page 21

REGENCY RESTAURANT

Downtowner Motor Inn, 201 West Oglethorpe Ave., Savannah, GA 31402; (912) 233-2172.

Dinner at the Regency is a pleasing affair, with flickering candlelight, wines, and entrees of beef, seafood, and fowl, served in the luxurious, relaxed atmosphere of the 18th century. The crowning touch is a selection from the dessert cart, laden with Viennese tortes, strawberry cheesecake, and Georgia pecan pie. Savannahians and visitors also make the Regency a regular stop for old-fashioned Southern breakfast with ham, grits, and biscuits, and for a delicious luncheon.

REGENCY CHEESECAKE *(Fruit glazed)*

5 (8-ounce) packages cream
    cheese
1¹/₂ cups granulated sugar
¹/₂ cup cornstarch
1¹/₃ cups granulated sugar
2¹/₂ cups sour cream
7 eggs
2 ¹/₂ teaspoons lemon juice
1 (10-inch) or 2 (8-inch) white
    cake for base (from your
    favorite recipe or bakery)
Fruit glaze (see Glossary)

In a mixer using a paddle, cream 1¹/₂ cups sugar with cream cheese on low speed for 3 minutes. Blend cornstarch with 1¹/₃ cups sugar. Add to cream cheese mixture and blend 5 minutes more on low speed, scraping bowl down several times with spatula.

Divide sour cream into 4 equal parts. Add to mixture 1 part at a time on medium speed. Mix until smooth, scraping down bowl. Test for lumps with fingers.

Set mixer on high and add eggs, one at a time. Mix until smooth after each addition. Scrape bowl down. Add lemon juice, mix, and scrape bowl down.

Pour into 1 (10- by 3-inch) or 2 (8- by 3-inch) greased round pan(s). Place pan(s) in water bath (larger pan filled with water) and bake at 300 degrees F. for 1¹/₂ hours, or until cake starts to crack on top. Pan size will vary time in oven. Remove from oven and water bath. Cool slightly. When cool enough to handle, yet still hot (see Note) invert onto a like-size circle of white cake sliced one-half inch thick. Save crumbs from slicing cake. Chill overnight.

Top cake with a fruit glaze such as strawberry, blueberry, peach, etc. Brush sides of cake with honey or syrup. Press cake crumbs on cake sides using your hands. Place plated cake on left palm, pressing cake crumbs on with right palm and fingers.

Note: Cake will stick to pan if you wait for it to be cold. You must invert while cake is still very warm, yet cool enough to handle, about 135 degrees F.

MAKES 16 to 24 SERVINGS

SWAN COACH HOUSE

3130 Slaton Drive NW, Atlanta, GA 30305; (404) 261-0636.

After walking awe-struck through the antique-filled rooms of the Swan House and the Tullie Smith House and grounds, Atlantans and visitors from all over the world are ready to relax over a quiet luncheon in The Swan Coach House. Formerly the servants' quarters for the Swan House, The Coach House now serves delightful soups, sandwiches, and entrees. Atlanta ladies especially cherish The Coach House, and enjoy browsing the gift shop and gallery, operated by the Forward Arts Foundation.

LEMON CHESS PIE

1¹/₄ cups cake flour
¹/₂ teaspoon salt
6 tablespoons shortening, cold
3 tablespoons ice water, about
Grated rind and juice of 3 lemons
9 large eggs
2¹/₄ cups sugar
1¹/₂ tablespoons margarine or
    butter, melted
3 tablespoons milk
¹/₈ teaspoon salt

Sift the flour with the salt. Cut in the shortening until mixture is mealy. Lifting mixture with fork add ice water and grated lemon rind, until it holds together.

Form into a ball and chill for about 30 minutes. Roll out the dough, using extra flour for handling. Fit loosely into a (10-inch by 1¹/₂-inch deep) pie pan. Flour the bottom of 1 more pie pan and place on top of the pastry. Weight it down with raw rice or dried beans, and bake at 400 degrees F. until golden brown, 15 to 20 minutes. Remove top pan.

Combine eggs, sugar, margarine, milk, and salt. Beat vigorously with a wire whisk, at least 30 licks 5 times at 5 minute intervals. Add lemon juice just before pouring into baked pie shell. Bake at 350 degrees F. for approximately 35 minutes.

The secret is in the baking. The center of the pie should be just a little shaky when removed from oven. It should be slightly brown. If it browns too much before getting done, invert your other pie pan and place on top.

Let cool before cutting.

MAKES 1 PIE OR 8 SERVINGS

TOULOUSE

Colony Square Hotel, Peachtree & 14th Sts. NE, Atlanta, GA 30361; (404) 892-6000.

Toulouse, a romantic candlelit hideaway in the Colony Square Hotel, proudly reigns as one of the Southeast's finest French restaurants. Enhanced by fine wines, dinner at Toulouse opens with hors d' oeuvres, and moves silkenly through soups, salad, an intermezzi of calvados sorbet in individual carved ice swans, classical French entrees rich with sauces, and the grand finale — Grand Marnier souffle, chocolate mousse, or French pastries as light as a cloud.

GRAND MARNIER SOUFFLE

2/3 cup milk
4 egg yolks
5 tablespoons sugar
1 1/2 tablespoons flour
4 tablespoons Grand Marnier
6 egg whites

In the top of a double boiler over hot water, heat milk.

Beat the egg yolks with sugar until mixture becomes light yellow. Add the flour, and then add milk. Return to top of double boiler and cook slowly until mixture thickens. Stir frequently with wooden spoon. Let cool.

Butter inside of a souffle dish and coat with sugar.

Add Grand Marnier to cold souffle mixture.

Beat egg whites until they form stiff peaks. Very gently fold egg whites into souffle mixture.

Fill souffle dish to the rim and bake at 400 degrees F. for approximately 15 to 20 minutes. Serve immediately.

MAKES 4 SERVINGS

BAILEY'S IRISH CREAM MOUSSE

3 $1/2$ cups milk
6 egg yolks
$1/2$ cup sugar
2 small ($1/4$-ounce) packages
  gelatin, softened in water
1 cup Bailey's Irish Cream
4 cups cream, whipped

Reserve $3/4$ cup milk. Scald, remaining milk. Mix reserved cold milk well with egg yolks and sugar. Pour into hot milk and cook over low heat, stirring until mixture will coat a spoon. Stir in soaked gelatin and cool.

When the custard begins to set, stir until smooth. Pour in Bailey's Irish Cream, fold in whipped cream, and pour into mold or individual glasses at once.

Chill and serve.

MAKES 12 SERVINGS

UPSTAIRS AT GENE & GABE'S

Gene & Gabe's Restaurant, 1582¹/₂ Piedmont Ave, NE, Atlanta, GA 30324; (404) 892-2261.

After a splendid Northern Italian dinner downstairs at Gene & Gabe's Restaurant, come Upstairs to Atlanta's lively New York-style cabaret. Every seat's excellent in this cozy theater, which features first-rate performers in satirical and musical comedy revues. Shows are usually original works, with a repertoire that changes every six weeks. For one of Atlanta's most exciting and sophisticated evenings of live entertainment, this is the number one address.

STRAWBERRIES CHANTILLY

1 quart fresh strawberries
1 pint Marsala wine
1 cup sugar, confectioners
    or granulated
1 pint heavy whipping cream
¹/₂ cup sugar
1 cup Cointreau or Grand Marnier

Remove stems from strawberries and wash. Pat dry with paper towel.
Marinate strawberries in Marsala wine and sugar for 3 hours.
Before serving, mix cream, sugar and Cointreau or Grand Marnier together until thick.
Serve plentifully over strawberries.

MAKES 6 SERVINGS

DAYBREAK RESTAURANT

Days Inn, 201 West Bay St., Savannah, GA 31401; (912) 236-4440.

In keeping with historic Savannah on the outside, but with a strikingly contemporary interior inside, this high-rise Days Inn sits facing the river. The DayBreak Restaurant offers 24-hour service of appetizing selections of American cuisine. Days Inn were born in 1970, and now these pleasant hotels, designed for travelers who insist on the best, can be found in 35 states from coast to coast, and even across the border in Canada.

THE DAYBREAKER

1 egg
¹/₂ cup milk
5 ounces fresh orange juice
1 scoop vanilla ice cream
2 tablespoons honey
1 orange slice

Crack egg into blender. Add milk and orange juice, then add ice cream and honey.
Place top on blender and blend for 35 to 40 seconds on high speed.
Pour into chilled 14-ounce glass and garnish with an orange slice on the rim of the glass.
MAKES 1 SERVING
Photograph, Page 21

"A man hath no better thing under the sun, than to eat, and to drink, and to be merry."

THE BIBLE, ECCLESIASTES CHAPTER VIII, VERSE 15.

CULINARY COMPLEMENTS

WINES

GEORGIA WINES

Georgians have sought to grow fine wine since General James Oglethorpe's colonists planted grapes in 1733 in Savannah. Their fine European vines (vitis vinifera) perished due to insects and bacteria. Resorting, therefore, to American grapes such as Muscadine and Concord, by 1880 Georgia had become the sixth largest wine producer in the U.S.A. In 1907 the state voted dry, squelching the grape industry until the 1930s when it was revived as a cash crop. In 1936, Monarch Wine Company opened in Atlanta to relieve the disastrous peach surplus and now produces over one million gallons of peach wine yearly.

The first commercial Georgia vinifera (European grapes) wine, 1981 Etowa Ridges Chardonnay, was grown by Gay Dellinger near Cartersville. In Georgia's 250th year two wineries are set to open: Chateau Elan, headed by Ed Friedrich, in Braselton; and B&B Rosser Winery near Athens. With modern vineyard techniques, vinifera has found a home in north Georgia after 250 years.

Georgia's per capita consumption in 1980 was 1.2 gallons, and is one of the fastest growing in the nation. Atlanta enjoys a national reputation for a burgeoning wine community and has chapters of all national wine groups. Other growing markets are Augusta, Savannah, Macon, and Columbus. The annual Atlanta Wine Festival, started in 1980, is a major September event.

MATCHING FOOD AND WINE

This guide offers a host of suggestions for basic food categories. As helpful and time-proven as these traditional accompaniments are, they are not shackles. Use them as springboards for launching new ideas of your own.

In the following guide, groups of food are matched predominately with groups of wine that are from California, Italy, and France, since those are the leading producers of wines consumed in the U.S.A., followed by Germany and others. If you cook with wine, always use good quality wine and serve it with that food.

DUCK, QUAIL, GAME BIRDS, TURKEY. Good with light red dry wines.
California—Pinot Noir, Burgundy, jug red table wine, Cabernet Sauvignon, Merlot.
Italy—Valpolicella, Chianti, Nebbiolo, Merlot.
France—Medoc, red Graves, St. Emilion, Cote de Beaune Villages, red Burgundy. Note, simple Rosé or Beaujolais-Village are best with Thanksgiving feasts, which are more vegetable than turkey dinners.

BEEF, LAMB, HEARTY/SPICY VEAL OR CHICKEN OR PASTA, BARBECUE, STRONG CHEESE. Dry red table wines.
California—Cabernet Sauvignon, Merlot, Zinfandel, Barbera, Charbono, Petite Syrah, Pinot Noir, Burgundy, jug reds.
Italy—Chianti Riserva, Nebbiolo, Barolo, Brunello de Montalcino, Gattinara, Bardolino, Grignolino, Merlot, Montepulciano de Abruzzo.
France—St. Julien, Pauillac, St. Emilion, Pomerol, Gevrey-Chambertin, Nuits St. George, Cote de Nuits Villages, Hermitage, Chateauneuf-du-Pape, jug red Bordeaux or red Burgundy.
Other—Cabernet Sauvignon from Romania, Bulgaria, South Africa, Australia; South African Pinotage; Australian Shiraz; red Rioja or Catalan from Spain; Marechal Foch, Leon Millot, New York State Burgundy from U.S.A.

LIGHT VEAL, CHICKEN, PORK ROAST. Generally light white wines, either dry or off-dry, or some light reds.

California—Chardonnay, Chablis, Sauvignon Blanc, brut Champagne, Gamay Beaujolais (light red).

Italy—Pinot Bianco, Pinot Grigio, Frascati, Soave.

France—white Bordeaux, Muscadet, Vouvray, Pouilly-Fume, Chablis, St. Veran.

Other—Qualitatswein or Kabinett quality wines from Germany; Vinho Verde from Portugal; Riesling from Alsace or Romania; white table wine from South Africa.

HEARTY VEAL, CHICKEN, PASTA, MILD CHEESE. Red or white wines with more body and robust flavors.

California—Merlot, Napa Gamay, Barbera, jug reds; Gewurztraminer, Fume Blanc, Chardonnay, jug whites.

Italy—Orvieto Secco, Corvo Bianco, Verdicchio (whites); Valpolicella, Chianti, Bardolino (reds).

France—Beaune, Beaujolais, jug red Bordeaux or Burgundy.

Other—dry white from Rioja or Catalan regions of Spain; Gewurztraminer from Alsace; Seyval Blanc, Vidal Blanc from U.S.A.

CRAB, LOBSTER, OYSTERS, TROUT. Dry white wines with high acidity or German Mosel wines which are off-dry but have high acidity. For rich fish such as salmon, a light red wine may work well.

California—Dry Riesling, Sauvignon Blanc, Brut Champagne, jug whites.

Italy—Pinot Grigio, Frascati, Corvo Bianco, Soave, Trebbiano.

France—Chablis, Pouilly-Fume, Sancerre, jug white Bordeaux.

Other—German Mosel or Rhein of Qualitatswein or Kabinett quality or Trocken (dry); white table wines from South Africa; Rieslings from Pacific Northwest, U.S.A.

LIGHT PASTA. Light white or red wines depending on power of sauce.

California—Chardonnay, Pinot Noir Blanc, dry Riesling.

Italy—Corvo Bianco, Orvieto Secco.

France—Chablis, Beaujolais.

Other—Seyval Blanc, Vidal Blanc from U.S.A.

HAM. Generally matched with rosé.

California—Grenache Rosé, Cabernet Rosé, Gamay, Rosé or Blanc of Pinot Noir, Gewurztraminer, jug rosé.

France—Tavel Rosé, Anjou Rosé. **Other**—Rosé from Italy or Portugal.

SPICY CHINESE, MEXICAN, PEPPERY BARBECUE. These powerful flavors can smother the taste of dry wine, leaving it tasting thin and bitter. Try chilled Gewurztraminers from Alsace or California, chilled Beaujolais from France or U.S.A., chilled Pinotage from South Africa, or best of all—beer.

SOUP. No wine is required, but it is delightful to serve a dry sherry with and in creamed soups. In many French country homes there is a custom of pouring about a spoonful of dry red wine into each person's bowl when their soup is nearly gone. The warmth of the bowl releases the wine's bouquet and makes the last spoonsful of soup taste even better.

DESSERTS. You may prefer a fine sweet wine either simply alone or with your dessert.

California—Sweeet Chenin Blanc; sweet Riesling; late harvest wines from grapes such as Riesling, Gewurztraminer, or Zinfandel; Port; Cream Sherry; sparkling Moscato or Chenin Blanc; fruit wines such as Blackberry.

Italy—Asti Spumante, Marsala.

France—Sauternes, Barsac, sweet Champagne, sparkling Muscat.

Germany—Rieslings from the Spatlese, Auslese, Beerenauslese, or Trockenbeere-nauslese categories.

Other—Portugal's Port; sweet Oloroso or Cream Sherry from Spain; Bual or Malmsey Madiera; Concord or Catawba from New York State.

BOLD EXPERIMENTS. There are trendy new flavor combinations springing up, such as light red wine with fish. Chocolate, long shunned as a wine accompaniment now is being seen served with red Burgundy or Pinot Noir. Sweet wines are considered poor food-companions, yet in the Sauternes and Barsac regions of France, the winemakers serve them with melon as an appetizer, with pâté instead of the traditional Champagne-and-pâté pairing, and with lamb. German wines are sometimes ignored because of their delicacy and light sweetness, but these wines do very well with fish because of their high acidity, and with light meals and snacks because of their crisp fruity flavors. By all means, experiment and search for new pairings.

DIET WINES. Wines labeled "light" list calorie information; most are around 57 calories per 100 milliliters (about 3.8 ounces). Since alcohol is the main source of wine calories, these wines have low alcohol content (8 to 9%). They also have low or no residual sugar, a further culling of calories. German Trocken wines are low in alcohol but they do not list calorie information. To roughly estimate wine calories, take the percent of alcohol listed on the label, double it to determine "proof" and that is the number of calories per ounce. At 12% alcohol, or 24 proof, a wine has 24 calories per ounce, plus calories from any sweetness. (This formula is not accurate enough for people who must strictly measure sugar intake.)

HOW TO READ THE LABEL

The number one question consumers ask is whether the wine is sweet or dry, and yet most labels do not specify it in so many words, although jug wine producers are getting better at providing this information. The truth is, many people talk dry wine and then drink sweet wine, an irony brought about by a lack of wine vocabulary and a false image of prestige accorded dry wines. The largest category of wine consumed by Americans is American white and rosé jug wines, which tend to have a slight sweetness. Truly dry wines are generally too harsh for casual wine drinkers. Further, there is a range from about .05 to 1.0% of sugar in wine where a person's ability to detect the slight sweetness influences their perceiving the wine as sweet or dry. Each person should rely on her/his own palate and decide each wine on its own merits and price value.

What a label will tell you is who made the wine, where, when, and from what grapes or in what style (such as American winemakers borrowing the French terms Burgundy, Chablis, or Champagne.) The name by which the wine is ultimately called can be either the name of a grape (Cabernet Sauvignon), a place (St. Emilion), a region (Sonoma County), a vineyard (Robert Young Vineyard), or a name the producer made up as a proprietary name (Hearty Burgundy).

Vintage dates do not certify quality, they only mean the grapes were harvested in that year, and any year can produce a poor, good, or fabulous crop.

YOUR WINE CELLAR

A wine cellar might really be in your cellar, but it may be in your closet or in the dining room or anywhere you have space. A wine cellar is first and simply a storage space that is cool, dark, and undisturbed. Second it is a source of convenience, a cache of handy wine. Third it is an attractive investment, not in financial dividends, but in psychic dividends of tasting a properly matured wine.

Lay all bottles, including Port and Champagne, on their sides flat enough to keep the corks wet and swollen, but not enough to let sediment collect in the bottle shoulder or neck. Jug wines should not be cellared; drink them within a few weeks or months while still fresh.

All wine has life curve. It is born in fermentation, endures adolescence in barrels or bottles, and in bottles it matures to its prime, then declines and loses all allure. For some like light, fruity, red Nouveau Beaujolais, this takes only a few months. For others like robust, tannic Cabernet Sauvignon it can take decades. While the best red table wines outlive the best white table wines, age does not bene-fit all reds, nor destroy all whites.

HOW COLD IS CHILLED?

It is a national crime that we drink our red wines too warm and white wines too cold. The taste of a warm red wine is not at all refreshing and leaves your mouth feeling like flocked wallpaper. What remorse springs from enduring a glass of white wine so cold it makes your teeth recede, only to discover it has warmed and released its bouquet and flavor just as you take the last sip? If you must err, do so in favor of cold and then warm the wine in the glass. In the refrigerator wine drops about 5 degrees per hour, faster in icy water.

DRY RED WINE should be served at 60 to 65 degrees F.
LIGHTER RED WINE AND DRY WHITE WINE: 55 to 60 degrees F.
LIGHTER WHITE WINE, VINTAGE CHAMPAGNE, SWEET SHERRY, SAUTERNES: 50 to 55 degrees F.
OTHER CHAMPAGNES AND SPARKLING WINES, DRY SHERRY: 45 to 50 degrees F.

Thermometers are available in some wine stores, wine-making supply shops, or you can get them through a wine accessories company.

HOW MUCH IS ENOUGH?

Wine is a beverage of moderation. A serving of wine is 3 to 4 ounces (100 milliliters). If you are serving a different wine with each course, one bottle can serve 8 people allowing 3 ounces each. Using the same wine throughout the meal, allow one-half to a full bottle of wine per person, depending on their fondness for wine and the length of the dinner.

LEFTOVER WINE

Yes, there will be leftover wine. Give it a second chance, don't pour it out. Recork the bottle, refrigerate, and serve the next day, or use it within a week in a sauce, stew, casserole, or roast. Take advantage of the economy of jug wines by pouring into clean, smaller bottles with screw tops, such as those for club soda, and use over the next few weeks (especially handy when cooking for only one or two people).

WINE GLASSES

Each style of wine shows its best features of color, bouquet, and taste in specific styles of stemmed glassware. Buy the thinnest, clearest stemware you can, starting with at least a dozen all-purpose glasses which hold about 8 to 10 ounces of wine. Choose a tulip-shaped bowl, or rounder, so you can swirl the wine without sloshing it. These will suffice for red or white wine. In a restaurant, a glass of house wine served from the bar may be 6 to 8 ounces so the glass is quite full. If poured from a bottle at the table, or in your home, a glass should be about one-third full only. This leaves air space for the wine's bouquet to develop and rise.

Dee Stone

Dee Stone
Wine Columnist, Atlanta **Journal & Constitution**
Editor, **The Arbor** Wine Magazine

FLUTE CHAMPAGNE • ALL PURPOSE • RED WINE • SHERRY OR PORT • WHITE WINE

TIPS FOR ENTERTAINING

Entertaining begins with an invitation, a request to share time and space in our homes; and the central element upon which all our entertaining builds is the common meal. Preparing for this meal, presenting it to our guests, and savoring it together is a caring and creative process. Literally, to entertain means to "hold among" and the key to successful entertaining is the host's understanding of himself as master of the ceremony of dining. In this sense there is a chef in each of us, a chief of cooking who wishes to orchestrate the sensuous delights of food — for friends.

The beauty of this role is that no two cooks are alike; each will produce different and exciting results, even from the same recipe. This is what makes the regional variations in national cuisines and creates the pride taken in further individualizing a special dish to the point of calling it by your own name.

PLAN YOUR MENU

Planning the menu is the first step toward preparation. The number of guests will determine the proportions of food. What kind of meal will you offer? International fare? Home cooking? Formal or casual? A special occasion, celebration or festival? Fresh seasonal foods? Your guest list will suggest the theme you want to set and your choice of courses from appetizer through dessert. Strive for a rhythm of courses that flow into one another with ease and some surprise. The idea is to have the whole meal unfold in marvelous sequence.

Weather conditions may affect your menu planning decisions. Hearty, steaming stews and soups may fit the winter cold, whereas poached fish and a light salad may be more suitable for summertime. Fresh seasonal foods should not be missed; for instance, be alert when asparagus is available in summer, when the oyster season starts in the fall, and when fruits are ripe and aromatic. Avoid using the same food in two different ways in one meal. An example is tomato soup and tomato aspic. Once around is enough; twice around is repetitious.

Make a shopping list of every ingredient required of each recipe on your menu. Don't forget your shopping list should also include necessary supplies such as ice, candles, fresh-cut flowers, mixes, herbs, wines, liqueurs, beverages, coffees, and garnishes. Give particular notice to flowers or greens to adorn your table and complement recipes with suitable and imaginative wine choices (see Wine Section). Wine is meant for food and food is meant for wine and man is meant for both.

TEST YOUR RECIPES

One basic rule chefs observe is "test your recipe" before serving it to guests. This will give you confidence when trying something new and shorten the time needed in preparation the day of the party.

PREPARATION IS THE KEY

Set the tempo of your preparation time to coordinate cooking the food, selecting the serving pieces and wines, sprucing up the house, polishing brass and silver, arranging flowers or decorations, and having yourself ready as an eager and receptive host. Make a detailed schedule for the day before the party. Rank order the cooking times of the dishes so that the oven is not used at the same time for two incompatible foods like a rib roast and a pie.

Some foods can be prepared ahead of time, even frozen, so the day of entertaining can be set aside for those additions that can only be done at the last minute. Have your kitchen neatly organized for the party day, especially the kitchen counters, so that moving food from stove or refrigerator to serving dishes to table is efficient and worry-free. Allow yourself a leisurely bath and ample dressing time before guests arrive.

Let food preparation be a culinary adventure. Enjoy taking the raw product of foods and translating them through your recipes and your own senses into very special forms and unique presentations.

FOOD COLOR, SHAPE, TEXTURE AND SIZE

Be aware of color combinations, avoid a monotone of color and seek color contrasts on each plate. No white cauliflower and whipped potatoes on the same plate, please. Brighten dark meats with yellow and green vegetables. Give salads subtlety and richness by introducing selected greens in the same bowl— perhaps a pale green Boston lettuce along with deep green spinach or red leaf lettuce.

Be attentive to individual food shapes and how they interface with other shapes; again look for contrast to heighten visual interest. A vegetable such as carrots can be sliced lengthwise into long strips, julienned into matchsticks, shaved into discs, or cut into chunks of varying thickness.

Be conscious of textures, in each fruit, vegetable, meat, seafood, and in the series of courses, in soups and appetizers, in entrees, in salads, and in desserts. Complement a crusty surface with a velvety sauce, pair soft with stiff, invent new marriages of traditional combinations, like pork and fruit.

Finally consider the size of each serving, being careful not to overload or undersell one component. You lose the balance of the parts if one is too weighty and another too skimpy. Satisfy your guests' request for special portions—a slim slice of cake, a healthy serving of meat. Appetites vary from person to person, between men and women. Your goal is to provide a meal enhanced by its own image, its presentation and one that leaves your guests pleasantly fulfilled, not overly stuffed.

FINESSE WITH GARNISHES

Garnishes provide light humor, visual sparkle, and finesse to food presentation. Be sure they do not obscure the food itself or mask the flavor. They are meant to be discriminating decoration, just the right amount, pointing to the sensuality of the food, enlivening that encounter. A sprinkle of paprika, a twig of watercress, a spear of endive, a small cluster of grapes, a wedge of lime — garnishes are the finishing touches in your presentation.

SELECTING SERVING PIECES

Today there is great versatility and exchange in the use of serving pieces and utensils. New materials and contemporary designs, glass, wood, pottery, steel, and enamel have joined the elder serving dishes of silver, china, and crystal. Here are some samples of the many possibilities in selecting serving pieces. Salad can be seen from the bottom up in a glass salad bowl and in a wooden bowl it appears almost as a verdant plant. The pale green of spinach soup will be heightened in a white soup bowl, a vichyssoise will be enriched in blue, green, or brown bowls. Whole fish is well displayed in long slender platters; breads can be served in a variety of baskets, wood bowls, boards, pottery, or silver bread dishes.

Choose your serving dishes well with an eye for color, shape, texture, and size. The foods should be comfortable in their serving dishes. At the moment guests come into the dining room the overall effect of the table with all in place should be a dramatic delight to all the senses.

WHEN GUESTS ARRIVE

Allow about an hour if you plan to serve cocktails or wine before dinner. This is a social time to gather in friends, give a gracious period for late arrivals, and enjoy the first fruits of seeing one another again and/or meeting new friends. A demitasse of hot or cold soup or an antipasto can be served in the living room as a prelude to the main course.

The ritual of entertaining is as old as breaking bread. In the generosity of giving a meal and becoming your own chef, you, too, are nourished in body and spirit.

Jean Thwaite
Food Writer Atlanta **Constitution**
Winner 1982 Vesta Award

BASIC STOCKS

BROWN STOCK. Place 6 pounds of marrow bones and two short ribs in pot with 4 quarts water. Add 1 cup drained canned tomatoes, 3 large carrots, 4 stalks celery, 1 large onion, 2 sprigs parsley, 1 bay leaf, 1 leek if available, pepper and salt to taste. Bring to a boil, reduce heat, and simmer for 2 to 3 hours. Strain and cool uncovered. When cool remove all fat that comes to top. Refrigerate or freeze in small containers for use as needed.

CHICKEN STOCK. Place about 4 pounds of chicken parts (backs, wings, and necks will do) in 4 quarts water. Add two medium whole onions, five stalks celery, three large carrots, one leek if available, pepper, 1 teaspoon salt (more if desired). Simmer for two to three hours. Strain and cool uncovered. When cool remove all fat that comes to top. Refrigerate or freeze in small containers for use as needed.

FISH STOCK. Heat 1/4 cup olive oil in pot, saute 1 chopped small onion until golden. Add 1 small clove garlic, 1/4 cup white wine, 2 quarts water, fresh herbs (such as tarragon or thyme), sprig fresh parsley, one stalk celery, two carrots, pinch nutmeg, salt and pepper to taste. Add 1 1/2 pounds fish heads and bones (these are available in any market from the butcher and usually are complimentary) and cook for 45 minutes to 1 hour. Strain through fine cheesecloth twice to make sure no bones get through. After straining, 1/4 cup butter may be melted in stock for extra richness. Cool uncovered, place in small containers, and refrigerate or freeze for future use.

VEAL STOCK. Place 4 pounds of veal knuckles or other veal bones and 1 pound beef bone with marrow in large pot with 2 quarts of water. Add 1 small onion, 1 bay leaf, 4 cloves, 3 sprigs parsley, 1 teaspoon thyme,, 2 stalks celery with leaves, 2 medium carrots, and salt and pepper to taste. Bring to a boil, reduce heat, and simmer for 2 to 3 hours. Strain, cool covered, and refrigerate or freeze.

BASIC SAUCES

BEARNAISE SAUCE. *A classic sauce traditionally served with grilled red meat, but sometimes with fish, chicken, or eggs.* Simmer 2 chopped shallots, 1 sprig chervil chopped, 1 sprig tarragon chopped, and 2 peppercorns in 4 tablespoons wine vinegar or white wine until all but 2 teaspoonfuls of vinegar or wine have evaporated. Strain and cool.
Put 2 egg yolks in top of double boiler over simmering water. Whisk wine mixture into them. Slowly whisk in 1/4 cup butter, cut into little pieces, until mixture resembles mayonnaise. If sauce curdles, remove from heat and vigorously whip in a teaspoon of cold water. *MAKES ABOUT 1 CUP.*

BORDELAISE SAUCE. *A French sauce for grilled meats.* Melt 2 tablespoons butter in saucepan. Add 2 tablespoons minced shallots and cook until transparent. Add 1/4 cup dry red wine and continue to cook until reduced by one-half. Then add in 1 1/2 cups brown sauce or canned beef gravy, 2 tablespoons lemon juice, 2 tablespoons minced parsley, salt and freshly ground white pepper to taste, 1/2 cup sliced mushrooms, sauted in butter optional, and heat through. *MAKES ABOUT 2 CUPS.*

BROWN SAUCE. *Also called Espagnole Sauce, one of the most versatile of the French basic sauces. Trouble to prepare, but may be frozen.* Preheat oven to 475 degrees F. Combine 5 pounds veal bones, 1 large onion chopped, 1 clove, 5 small carrots peeled and quartered, 2 stalks celery chopped including leaves, 1/2 tablespoon thyme, 1 teaspoon peppercorns crushed, 3 bay leaves, 3 cloves garlic not peeled, and 1 tablespoon salt in large roasting pan. Bake 45 minutes in oven, reducing heat if necessary, to keep bones from burning. Sprinkle with 1/2 cup flour and bake 15 minutes more.
Place ingredients in large kettle and add 2 cups water to roasting pan. Place over low heat, stirring to dissolve brown particles on bottom and sides of pan. Add to kettle and add remaining water, 1 1/4

cups tomato puree if desired, ¹/₂ cup leek tops chopped, and 3 sprigs parsley. Bring to boil, then reduce heat to simmer. Simmer for 2 hours, adding more liquid if necessary.

Skim to remove fat and foam as it rises to surface. Cool and strain.

Freeze, defrosting as necessary. Will keep tightly covered in refrigerator for 2 weeks.

DRAWN BUTTER. *A sauce similar to white sauce.* Melt ³/₄ cup butter in top of double boiler over hot water. Add 2 tablespoons flour and stir to combine. Add 2 cups water and season with salt and pepper to taste. Let it simmer until it thickens, stirring to keep it smooth. Slowly add 1 tablespoon butter, beating continuously until sauce becomes white. Add 2 tablespoons lemon juice. Stir and strain before serving.

HOLLANDAISE SAUCE. *A popular sauce, similar to Bearnaise sauce, made from eggs, butter, and lemon juice. A quick version may be made in a blender.* Place 3 egg yolks at room temperature, 2 tablespoons lemon juice at room temperature, ¹/₄ teaspoon salt, and pinch cayenne in blender. Turn on low speed for two seconds.

Heat ¹/₂ cup butter until bubbling but not brown. Turn blender on low speed and gradually add butter. Blend about 15 seconds or until sauce is thickened and smooth.

MADEIRA SAUCE. *Classical French wine sauce.* Melt 2 tablespoons butter in saucepan. Saute 2 tablespoons scallions or shallots, finely minced for 5 minutes, but do not allow butter to brown. Add 1¹/₂ cups brown sauce or canned beef gravy and 2 tablespoons lemon juice.

Bring to boil, add ¹/₄ cup Madeira wine, and simmer 5 minutes. *MAKES ABOUT 1¹/₄ CUPS.*

SEAFOOD SAUCE. Melt 1 cup butter in heavy large saucepan until bubbly. Add 2 cups flour and stir to combine. Gradually add 1 quart milk, stirring constantly, until mixture thickens and is smooth. Season with salt and white pepper to taste. Add 4 cubes Knorr's Swiss Fish Stock base that has been dissolved in a small amount of boiling water, 1 cup whipping cream, and ¹/₄ cup sherry.

TOMATO SAUCE. Heat 3 tablespoons olive oil in pan, add 1 clove garlic and 1 whole small onion. Lightly brown. Add 2 (6-ounce) cans tomato puree and 1 bay leaf. Simmer at least 1 hour. Remove garlic, onion, and bay leaf.

For richer sauce a short rib or other meat may be browned with onion and cooked in tomato sauce.

For seasoned sauce add fresh or dried herbs of choice.

WHITE SAUCE. *A liquid seasoning for food, also known as Bechamel, and probably the most important sauce of all as it is the basis for countless dishes.*

Medium White Sauce. Melt 2 tablespoons butter, but do not brown, over moderate heat. Add 2 tablespoons flour and stir until well blended. Use a wooden spoon or wire whisk. Heat 1 cup milk almost to a boil and add all at once to flour and butter, stirring vigorously. It will thicken when it comes to a boil. Simmer for about 5 minutes. Add salt and white pepper to taste.

Thin White Sauce. Use 1 tablespoon each butter and flour for 1 cup milk.

Thick White Sauce. Use 3 tablespoons each butter and flour for 1 cup milk.

GLOSSARY

AL DENTE. *"To the teeth," an adjective describing food, usually pastas or rice, that is firm to the bite, in contrast to food cooked until soft throughout.*

BASES. *Concentrated powders or cubes to be added to chicken, beef, or seafood dishes or to be reconstituted with water to make broths or stocks. Commercially available.*

BEARNAISE SAUCE. *See Basic Sauces.*

BECHAMEL. *See Basic Sauces under White Sauce.*

BLANCH. *To cook an ingredient briefly in a large amount of boiling water to set color or flavor of a vegetable, to loosen skin of fruit or vegetable, to remove excess salt, or to precook. Often used when it is desirable for ingredients to remain firm. Depending on vegetable, cook approximately 30 seconds to 2 minutes.*

BORDELAISE SAUCE. *See Basic Sauces.*

BOUILLON. *A clear soup or broth, made from various kinds of meat, where the fat has been removed from the stock. Also available in cubes to be reconstituted.*

BROWN SAUCE. *Also Espagnole sauce. A rich sauce made using trimmings of raw veal and ham, or rabbit, pork or game, seasonings and stock or bouillon. The stock may be made from meat, poultry, and fish, their bones, and from vegetables and seasonings. See Basic Sauces.*

BUTTERFLY. *To cut partially through and spread open to increase the surface area of food, e.g. shrimp.*

CEPES. *Large mushrooms grown in France and canned for export markets, often in olive oil or some other sauce, and they have a somewhat stronger flavor than the common mushroom. Cap is six inches or more in diameter and yellowish or reddish in color.*

CHANTERELLE. *French name for small edible yellow mushroom.*

CLARIFIED BUTTER. *Butter that has been gently heated and strained so that the whitish deposit is left behind.*

DEGLAZE. *To add liquid to the crusty bits left in a saute pan to dissolve them, usually done over heat. This adds flavor to many dishes.*

DEMI-GLACE. *Sauce made from one cup of glace de viande (see below), added to 2 cups brown sauce, simmered over low heat until reduced by half. It should be of a consistency to "half glaze" or coat food.*

DEVEIN. *Commonly refers to cleaning the small black filament from the back of a fish or prawn either before or after cooking.*

DRAWN BUTTER. *See Basic Sauces.*

EGG WASH. *A combination of eggs and water, one egg to one tablespoon water, which when brushed on pastry encourages even browning. It can also be used to seal one piece of pastry to another.*

FISH STOCK AND BOUILLON POWDER. *See Bases.*

FLAME or FLAMBE. *To pour warmed alcoholic beverages such as brandy, whiskey, or rum over food to set fire to it for purpose of adding flavor.*

FOLD. *To gently incorporate one food stuff into another without breaking it, particularly egg white which needs to remain frothy. If beaten, rather than folded, the froth would be broken down.*

GLACE DE VIANDE. *A concentrated stock obtained by reducing beef broth or stock.*

GLAZE. *A stock that is reduced until it coats the back of a spoon. Also a shiny coating, such as syrup, applied to a food. Also to make a food shiny or glossy by coating it with a glaze or by browning under a broiler in a hot oven.*

HOLLANDAISE SAUCE. *See Basic Sauces.*

JULIENNE. *To cut into small, thin strips, about one-eighth by one-eighth by two-and-a-half inches.*

KITCHEN BOUQUET. *A vegetable-based browning and seasoning sauce.*

LOBSTER BASE. *See Bases.*

LOBSTER, TO CLEAN. *If the lobster is alive, place lobster on its back on a cutting board and pierce head with a firm thrust of a French knife to kill it quickly. Bring the knife down through the center of the lobster to split in half. With both hands, crack the back of the shell by spreading the lobster open. Pull out and discard the stomach, a sac just behind the eyes. If desired, remove the tomalley (see next page) for use in stuffing. With a sharp blow of the back of the knife, crack the claws. The lobster is now ready for broiling.*

MADEIRA SAUCE. *See Basic Sauces.*

MARINATE, MARINADE. *To marinate food in a marinade is to soak food for a period of time in a highly seasoned liquid to impart flavor as well as to tenderize it. A marinade often includes wine, vinegar, olive oil, lemon peel and juice, salt, pepper, bay leaves, onions, thyme, parsley, cloves, garlic, and so forth.*

MEDALLIONS. *Small round or ovals of food, particularly of beef or veal, such as tournedos.*

MIREPOIX. *Cubes of uncooked carrots, onions, ham or pork (optional) barely sauted in butter with bay leaves and thyme. It is used as a garnish or a flavor enhancer to braised meat or poultry.*

MONOSODIUM GLUTAMATE. *A flavor enhancer sold under such names as MSG and ACCENT.*

MOREL. *An edible mushroom found in the springtime.*

NAP. *To coat a food with a rich white sauce, a procedure which is called napping or glazing.*

PERNOD. *An aromatic French liqueur, available in liquor stores.*

PHYLLO. *A papery-thin pastry used in many Greek and Middle Eastern dishes. Difficult to make, but available in the frozen-food case of many grocery and gourmet stores.*

POACH. *To cook food in water or other liquid that is not actually bubbling, at a temperature of 160 to 180 degrees F.*

PRAWNS. *In the United States, large shrimp are often called prawns. In Britain, any shrimp 2 to 3 inches in length is called a prawn; the smaller size is a shrimp.*

PUFF PASTRY. *A flaky combination of flour and butter bound with water. A rather tedious and exacting procedure to make at home, it fortunately is generally available in frozen-food cases of most grocery stores, and is very good.*

REDUCE. *To simmer or boil liquid until quantity is decreased. Usually for purpose of concentrating flavors.*

ROUX. *A mixture of equal parts butter, or other fats, and flour cooked together for varying periods of time depending on its use. It is the thickening agent in sauces. The amount used depends on the amount of liquid to be thickened.*

SEAR. *To brown surface of food quickly at high temperature.*

SCALD. *To pour boiling water over an ingredient placed in a colander so that the water will immediately drain from it.*

SCALLOPINE. *Italian for small, thin pieces of meat (scallop), usually veal or fish, flattened and fried in butter.*

SHRIMP, TO COOK. *Shrimp may be peeled and deveined either before or after cooking. Whichever way, shrimp should be placed in boiling water and cooked until they begin to turn pink, about 5 to 15 minutes, depending on size. Drain immediately and run cold water over them to stop cooking process. The cooking water may be seasoned with commercial crab boil, lemon slices, bay leaf, and so forth.*

SIMMER. *To cook food in water or other liquid that is bubbling gently, about 185 to 200 degrees F.*

SIMPLE SYRUP. *Combine one quart water to two cups sugar and boil for five minutes. May be bottled and kept in the refrigerator.*

SOFT BALL. *Syrup that has reached 234 degrees F. To test for soft ball stage, drop a small quantity of syrup into chilled water. Soft ball stage has been reached when it forms a ball that does not disintegrate but flattens out of its own accord when picked up with the fingers.*

STOCKS. *See Basic Stocks.*

TOMALLEY. *The liver of lobster and some other shell fish.*

WATER BATH. *To cook food in a container of water (bain marie) to keep it hot and/or prevent if from drying out during cooking. Produces an even heat.*

WHITE SAUCE. *See Basic Sauces.*

WOK. *A multi-functional cooking pan, traditionally used for Chinese cooking to conserve energy and cook foods quickly. It can be used for steaming, stir-frying, deep-fat frying, braising, or stewing.*

EQUIVALENT MEASURES

MEASURE	EQUIVALENT
A few grains, dash, pinch, etc. (dry)	Less than $1/8$ teaspoon
Dash (liquid)	2 or 3 drops
1 tablespoon	3 teaspoons
1 fluid ounce	2 tablespoons or $1/8$ cup
$1/4$ cup	4 tablespoons or 2 fluid ounces
$1/3$ cup	$5 1/3$ tablespoons or 4 fluid ounces
$1/2$ cup	8 tablespoons
$3/4$ cup	12 tablespoons or 6 fluid ounces
1 cup	16 tablespoons or 8 fluid ounces
1 cup (liquid)	$1/2$ pint
1 pint	2 cups (liquid) or 16 fluid ounces
1 quart	2 pints or 32 fluid ounces
1 gallon	4 quarts
1 pound (dry)	16 ounces

INDEX BY RECIPE NAME

INDEX BY CATEGORY

S

INDEX BY RESTAURANT

NOTES

CHEFS' SECRETS ORDER FORM

MAIL TO: TRIPLE M COMPANY, P.O. Box 720114, Atlanta, GA 30358.

Please send me _____ copies of *CHEFS' SECRETS FROM GREAT RESTAURANTS IN GEORGIA* @ only $12.95 per copy, which includes postage and handling. (Add appropriate state sales tax if mailed in Georgia.) Enclosed is my check or money order made out to Triple M Company for $_____, or credit card information.

NAME_____ TELEPHONE NUMBER_____

ADDRESS_____

CITY_____ STATE_____ ZIP_____

AMERICAN EXPRESS #_____ Exp. Date_____

VISA #_____ Exp. Date_____

MASTERCARD #_____ Exp. Date_____

SIGNATURE _____

Allow approximately 6 weeks for delivery. Add $3.00 per copy for orders from Canada and $6.00 per copy for orders outside North America.

CHEFS' SECRETS ORDER FORM

MAIL TO: TRIPLE M COMPANY, P.O. Box 720114, Atlanta, GA 30358.

Please send me _____ copies of *CHEFS' SECRETS FROM GREAT RESTAURANTS IN GEORGIA* @ only $12.95 per copy, which includes postage and handling. (Add appropriate state sales tax if mailed in Georgia.) Enclosed is my check or money order made out to Triple M Company for $_____, or credit card information.

NAME_____ TELEPHONE NUMBER_____

ADDRESS_____

CITY_____ STATE_____ ZIP_____

AMERICAN EXPRESS #_____ Exp. Date_____

VISA #_____ Exp. Date_____

MASTERCARD #_____ Exp. Date_____

SIGNATURE _____

Allow approximately 6 weeks for delivery. Add $3.00 per copy for orders from Canada and $6.00 per copy for orders outside North America.

CHEFS' SECRETS ORDER FORM

MAIL TO: TRIPLE M COMPANY, P.O. Box 720114, Atlanta, GA 30358.

Please send me _____ copies of *CHEFS' SECRETS FROM GREAT RESTAURANTS IN GEORGIA* @ only $12.95 per copy, which includes postage and handling. (Add appropriate state sales tax if mailed in Georgia.) Enclosed is my check or money order made out to Triple M Company for $_____, or credit card information.

NAME_____ TELEPHONE NUMBER_____

ADDRESS_____

CITY_____ STATE_____ ZIP_____

AMERICAN EXPRESS #_____ Exp. Date_____

VISA #_____ Exp. Date_____

MASTERCARD #_____ Exp. Date_____

SIGNATURE _____

Allow approximately 6 weeks for delivery. Add $3.00 per copy for orders from Canada and $6.00 per copy for orders outside North America.

ORDER OTHER CHEFS' SECRETS COOKBOOKS
Price $12.95 each, including postage and handling

NO.

_____ CHEFS' SECRETS FROM GREAT RESTAURANTS IN LOUISIANA   Available summer 83
       SPECIAL 1984 WORLD EXPOSITION EDITION

_____ CHEFS' SECRETS FROM GREAT RESTAURANTS IN CALIFORNIA   Available summer 83

_____ CHEFS' SECRETS FROM GREAT RESTAURANTS IN PENNSYLVANIA   Available summer 83

_____ CHEFS' SECRETS FROM GREAT RESTAURANTS IN THE NATION'S
       CAPITAL   Available fall 83

_____ CHEFS' SECRETS FROM GREAT RESTAURANTS IN CANADA   Available fall 83

Fill out front of order form and mail with check or money order or credit card information to: TRIPLE M COMPANY, P.O. Box 720114, Atlanta, GA 30358. (For information on other cookbooks in the series, write to TRIPLE M.)

ORDER OTHER CHEFS' SECRETS COOKBOOKS
Price $12.95 each, including postage and handling

NO.

_____ CHEFS' SECRETS FROM GREAT RESTAURANTS IN LOUISIANA   Available summer 83
       SPECIAL 1984 WORLD EXPOSITION EDITION

_____ CHEFS' SECRETS FROM GREAT RESTAURANTS IN CALIFORNIA   Available summer 83

_____ CHEFS' SECRETS FROM GREAT RESTAURANTS IN PENNSYLVANIA   Available summer 83

_____ CHEFS' SECRETS FROM GREAT RESTAURANTS IN THE NATION'S
       CAPITAL   Available fall 83

_____ CHEFS' SECRETS FROM GREAT RESTAURANTS IN CANADA   Available fall 83

Fill out front of order form and mail with check or money order or credit card information to: TRIPLE M COMPANY, P.O. Box 720114, Atlanta, GA 30358. (For information on other cookbooks in the series, write to TRIPLE M.)

ORDER OTHER CHEFS' SECRETS COOKBOOKS
Price $12.95 each, including postage and handling

NO.

_____ CHEFS' SECRETS FROM GREAT RESTAURANTS IN LOUISIANA   Available summer 83
       SPECIAL 1984 WORLD EXPOSITION EDITION

_____ CHEFS' SECRETS FROM GREAT RESTAURANTS IN CALIFORNIA   Available summer 83

_____ CHEFS' SECRETS FROM GREAT RESTAURANTS IN PENNSYLVANIA   Available summer 83

_____ CHEFS' SECRETS FROM GREAT RESTAURANTS IN THE NATION'S
       CAPITAL   Available fall 83

_____ CHEFS' SECRETS FROM GREAT RESTAURANTS IN CANADA   Available fall 83

Fill out front of order form and mail with check or money order or credit card information to: TRIPLE M COMPANY, P.O. Box 720114, Atlanta, GA 30358. (For information on other cookbooks in the series, write to TRIPLE M.)